How to
Buy Money

How to Buy Money

*Investing Wisely
for Maximum Return*

Wayne F. Nelson

McGraw-Hill Book Company

New York   St. Louis   San Francisco

Toronto   Hamburg   Mexico

Library of Congress Cataloging in Publication Data

Nelson, Wayne F.
How to buy money.
1. Investments—Handbooks, manuals, etc.
2. Money market—Handbooks, manuals, etc.
I. Title.
HG4527.N44   332.6'78   81–3751
ISBN 0-07-046220-8   AACR2

Book design by Andrew Roberts

For Marti

my inspiration

my challenge

my life

Author's Note

How to Buy Money is written to help successful, fully occupied individuals who are not professional money managers make better decisions about managing their money.

Its premise is that such individuals do not have a great deal of time to worry about their finances. Thus, in order to make informed decisions about buying money, such individuals, like you perhaps, must have a sound, fundamental understanding of the ways to do it. If you know the basics, the task of turning your current cash into future income becomes manageable.

Wall Street's investment brokers are an imaginative bunch. They constantly develop and promote new investment programs. Despite the sophistication of the new proposals, each one has its roots in the traditional money markets that have existed for decades. Consider, for example, an operation called the *equity unit trust*. It is a closed-end, unmanaged portfolio of common stocks of utility companies with an optional discounted dividend reinvestment plan. If all of that gobbledygook is clear to you, you will be able to skip a number of chapters of this book. For most people, however, despite their business background or sophistication in their own area of expertise, that one-line description of an equity unit trust is not very helpful. Because in order to understand it, you need to know the definitions of these terms: *closed-end, unmanaged portfolio, common stocks, utility companies, optional dividend reinvestment plan, discount, equity* and *unit trust.*

And so, *How to Buy Money* will first lead you to the task of properly constructing your personal securities portfolio by helping you acquire the basic knowledge of securities that no thoughtful investor should be without.

The second purpose of *How to Buy Money* is to help you *manage* your investment portfolio. It will give you direction in putting together your personal investment program. Most people do an inadequate job of this. Again, it is not because they are unintelligent or unclever. Rather, it is because they are unprepared. No amount of grooming protects an investor from mistakes. No educational background trains people to invest their money. The best preparation for an investor is experience. The next best is the insight which permits an investor—you—to learn from the experience of others. *How to Buy Money* offers guidance gleaned from the experience of investment professionals about how to use financial tools to your best advantage. In the Bibliography I will refer to classic investment books which will further broaden your knowledge if you care to read them. In this way, you can chart an investment education program that will prepare you to handle your investments with the same professional detachment and energy you use in your occupation.

There is no such thing as a totally safe way to buy money. For example, even if you buy money with U.S. government guaranteed bonds or a federally insured savings account, you are gambling on the future purchasing power of that money. Every investment involves some measure of risk. But there is an important difference between the concept of risk and the emotion called *fear.* They are not the same. Fear results from ignorance, from a lack of understanding or an inability to judge the unknown. Fear can paralyze an investor or cause him to avoid investment decisions. The world of money should be appreciated for the risks involved but never avoided because of fear. The final goal of *How to Buy Money* is to open up the world of money for people who fear it. An understanding of the pros and cons of each investment alternative will help dissipate your fear, give you a new perspective about investing, and allow you to become a citizen of the financial world capable of moving about in that world with genuine confidence.

Making your money grow is great fun. Choosing investments that work out well can bring you untold pleasure. Once you learn how to buy money, you open a world that can be one of the most exhilarating experiences of your life.

Contents

How to
Buy Money

1

How and Why to Buy Money

In my experience, many people seem to believe that the easiest way to manage money is to ignore it. Others worry about their finances with the zeal of Disraeli's father, who wrote to his son, "There seems to be the danger of a run on the banks. I think I will come up to London to take out my money as long *as it is not raining."*

While this painless form of money management is popular, it is extremely expensive. Simplicity, in this instance, should not be mistaken for excellence.

If you are like most of us, you spend your most fertile thinking moments of each day finding solutions to other people's problems. You exhaust your physical energies struggling with the minute-to-minute challenges of your occupation. And you ignore your personal financial life, or squeeze what little attention you give it into the end of the day when neither your mind nor your body is at its peak efficiency level.

Saturday morning when you are away from the office and your mind is fresh would be an ideal time to think about your personal financial strategy. Instead, you probably tire yourself out with some mundane house chores. The result: Your house is probably better cared for than your financial future.

This is balderdash! Give a neighborhood kid ten dollars to push your lawn mower around your yard or to dust the furniture. Take that time to sit in an easy chair and think about your personal financial situation. Think about how you can buy money with the money you have already saved. I promise you that the ideas that will come from this precious personal business time will be worth the ten dollars you paid the youngster to perform the mindless tasks.

Saving Money Is Buying Money

The act of saving money is the start of buying money, because money is never idle. Even though in your mind's eye your savings are sitting quietly in your checking or passbook savings account, in the mind of your banker, it is money to be actively managed. Your banker's job is to buy money with the money on deposit in his bank.

So while you are mowing your lawn and ignoring your savings account, your banker is hard at work making those dollars work as hard as he can on behalf of his bank. As agreed when you made your routine savings account deposit, the bank will pay you the interest to which you are entitled. Any amount the bank is able to earn above that belongs to the bank. Your bank is a master at buying money with your money and there is nothing wrong about that. *There is also nothing wrong with your becoming knowledgeable enough to buy more money for yourself.* And there is certainly nothing wrong with spending the extra time necessary to make certain that the dollars you have saved are buying as much money for you as they can.

Managing your cash is critically important. It is as important as managing your other investments—and no one is in a better position to do it than you! What you have to do is learn about the various tools that are available to help you and how to go about using them. The difference between using them and not using them is akin to standing at your window every morning and throwing money into the street.

As you can see, if you are saving money at a 12 percent rate instead of 9 percent, and you are saving $200 per month, you will have increased the power of your savings by more than $60,000 over a twenty-year period. Thus it is clear that the investor who can consistently buy money at even a percentage point higher rate of interest will fare substantially better over the long run. So spending the extra time to check up on your savings program *is* worthwhile. (See chart on page 9.)

Money Market Funds

The most popular and widely used savings account alternative is called a *money market fund.* Sylvia Porter has written, "To keep your savings in a regular passbook savings account when rates paid by money market funds are at high levels suggests apathy or abysmal ignorance."

This is a very strong statement, but sometimes it is necessary to club someone on the head to get his attention. If you are not using a money market fund when interest rates are high, consider yourself clubbed on the head. By not substituting a money market fund for your passbook savings account, you are coming as close to throwing money into the street as you probably ever will. What is a money market fund and why does it generate such high yields? When Uncle Sam, banks, and corporations need cash for a short period of time, they buy it in the "money market." Other institutions with cash to spare sell their money in this market. How much it costs to buy money in this market depends on the same supply and demand law that affects every other type of product with which you are familiar. When there is a lot of money available, the cost of buying that money will be cheap. When there is little money, its cost will be high.

The money market is the bazaar where multimillion-dollar transactions are commonplace. As an individual, it is not normally possible to participate in this fast-paced and very sophisticated market—unless you use a money market fund. A money market fund is a large pool of money that has been supplied in relatively small amounts by individuals and smaller corporations. The money is managed by a fund manager who is familiar with this marketplace. After subtracting some part of the interest earned for management and other fees (usually 1/2 of 1 percent), the balance is paid to the investors. For example, if the interest earned is 10 1/2 percent, the fund will pay you 10 percent. The rate of interest paid will change daily because the rate earned by the fund changes daily.

The rate changes because the securities purchased by the fund are constantly changing. They are all short-term securities, most of which will mature within thirty days. Some exist only overnight, others only over the weekend. Each will probably pay a different rate of interest as interest rates in the money market change constantly.

When all short-term interest rates are high, the investors in money market funds are able to earn a very attractive rate of return on the dollars invested. Remember, there is no guaranteed rate of interest. Rather, the rate fluctuates. If rates go up, your rate of return goes up. If they go down to the point where you could do better elsewhere, take your money out.

HOW TO INVEST IN A MONEY MARKET FUND

You can deal directly with the money market fund or through a stock broker. A complete and free list of available funds can be obtained through the Investment Company Institute, 1775 K Street, NW, Washington, D.C. 20006. And there are usually plenty of advertisements in the back pages of the *Wall Street Journal*. For ten dollars, William E. Donoghue of Holliston, Massachusetts, will send you a brochure that provides more extensive information, along with data on yields for the last two-and-a-half years.

The minimum deposit varies from fund to fund. It is usually not more than $5,000, although some funds can be started with as little as $1,000. Deposits and withdrawals of several hundred dollars are usually permitted and the money market funds can usually be drawn down to a few dollars, or even to zero, and still remain open. Most money market funds offer a check writing privilege that allows you to write checks provided they are for at least $500. There are usually no charges for any of these services. I say "usually" so often because it is difficult to generalize about the rules and requirements of each fund. Information about the fees as well as the type of short-term securities the fund will make with your dollars is spelled out in the prospectus. That document can be obtained without charge from any fund manager. Most money market funds have a toll-free number that can be used to ask questions about the fund and make withdrawals. Deposits can be made by mail.

If you use your stockbroker for your money market fund transactions, keep in mind that he is not paid for this service. As a result, most stockbrokers discourage overly frequent transactions.

WHAT IS THE RISK OF MONEY MARKET FUNDS?

Most people who choose not to use money market funds cite the fact that they are not protected by the Federal Deposit Insurance Corporation (FDIC), or the Federal Savings and Loan Insurance Corporation (FSLIC), as are savings accounts in banks and in savings and loan associations.

Money market funds are defined as "securities" according to the Securities Investor Protection Corporation (SIPC), the federally chartered organization that protects investors if their brokerage firm collapses. If you have cash or securities on deposit with a brokerage firm which is an SIPC member, by virtue of the fact you have invested in a money market fund, your investment will be protected. This does not mean, however, that if you invest in a money market fund which fails because the fund bought high risk securities you would get your money back. The protection insures only that you would receive your share of the securities, which might not be worth much—for if the securities were valuable, the fund wouldn't have failed.

5

You must make a judgment as to quality of the money market fund by examining the types of securities it buys as well as its investment criteria and limitations. In addition to U.S. government and bank notes, some funds invest in commercial paper (short-term borrowings by corporations) and bankers' acceptances (commercial bank borrowings linked to an international commercial transaction, guaranteed by both the bank and the corporation). Some money market funds invest only in U.S. government securities. The yield of these funds is somewhat lower, but there is little worry that Uncle Sam won't be able to make interest payments.

RISK VERSUS REWARD

Throughout the world of investing, there is the concept of risk versus reward. Every investor must understand this principal. Quite simply, the risk/reward concept says: the greater the risk, the higher the possible reward. This does not necessarily mean that just because the reward appears to be unusually high there must also be great risk. For example, the same U.S. government that buys your money at 7 1/2 percent interest with Series EE bonds may buy your money with its Treasury Bills at 12 percent interest. Both are guaranteed and risk free. *But if an investment return appears to be out of line with similar investments, then it should be a clue to you to be wary.* Everyone who needs money wants to buy it from you as cheaply as possible. So if you are offered an unusually high return, remember that your good judgment is not what is being appealed to, your greed or speculative nature may well be. If you are uncomfortable with any investment that is not federally insured or government guaranteed, then use a money market fund of U.S. government securities only. You will earn a percentage point or two less in interest, but you may sleep better at night. And that, in the long run, is your best possible investment.

There are two risks to owning a security: a *credit risk*, which is what we have been discussing, and the *risk of price fluctuation*. In nearly all money market funds, this risk is virtually nonexistent. Because the investments made by all money mar-

6

ket funds are very short term, the market price fluctuation of your investment will be minimal. Most funds establish the purchase price per share at one dollar and pay that amount per share when the shares are redeemed. If there is any market price fluctuation in the share value, it is accounted for by adjusting the amount of interest paid to you up or down.

MANY USES OF MONEY MARKET FUNDS

The ways in which investors can use money market funds are limited only by their imagination. Some physicians deposit their weekly receipts from their practices into a money market fund and then write money market checks to pay themselves and their larger bills at the end of each month. The difference in interest earned versus what they had been earning in a no-interest checking account is the equivalent of seeing and billing several additional patients each week. This system works equally well to help small corporations capitalize on their excess cash.

Some people write their quarterly Internal Revenue Service (IRS) payments on their money market fund checks. If Uncle Sam takes two weeks to cash their checks, they earn another two weeks of interest because interest is being credited to their accounts until their checks are cleared.

You may place an order with your broker to buy bonds that won't settle—that is, the money won't be required—for two or three weeks. Instead of allowing the money to sit in a passbook account at low interest until the settlement date, or at the brokerage firm at no interest, you could keep your money in the brokerage firm's money market fund.

NOW Accounts

These are interest-bearing checking accounts that allow your funds to earn interest until the checks written against those funds are presented. I've had people ask whether it makes sense to transfer money from a money market fund into a NOW account. The answer is that you should keep your money where it is earning the highest rate of interest. NOW accounts are paying 5 1/4 percent interest. Money market funds are substantially higher than that. Transfer only the money you immediately expect to write checks against from your money market fund into your NOW account.

CMA

Merrill Lynch offers an account it calls Cash Management. This is a money market fund against which you can write checks of any amount. Unlike the NOW account, which pays 5 1/4 percent interest, the Cash Management Account pays the higher money market fund rate. A tax-free CMA money market fund is also available. Three other features of CMA are:

1. Dividends and interest paid by your securities held in your Merrill Lynch account are automatically deposited into the CMA.
2. A special VISA card allows you to draw cash or borrow against the value of the securities in your Merrill Lynch brokerage account.
3. You can write checks against the value of your securities to the extent permitted. It is like writing a loan for yourself using your securities as collateral.

At present to qualify for the Cash Management Account you must have deposit cash or securities with a value of at least $20,000. At the time this is written, CMA is offered only by Merrill Lynch, but other brokerage firms are sure to follow.

This is the message: allowing your money to remain idle can be costly. Money market funds can create many extra dollars of income for you.

The Growing Power of Money

Does it make much of a difference to your long-range financial well-being if you are able to buy money at only one percentage

point or two higher? Absolutely! The following chart demon-
strates *why* you need to know as much as you can about *how* to
buy money. All totals shown on the chart do not include the
diminution that would be caused by taxes, which vary according
to each individual's tax bracket.

Annual Interest Rate (compounded monthly)	Amount of Monthly Savings	Twenty-Year Totals
9%	$200	$133,578.41
	500	333,946.04
	1,000	647,982.07
10%	$200	$151,872.04
	500	379,680.13
	1,000	759,360.13
11%	$200	$173,127.79
	500	432,819.47
	1,000	865,638.92
12%	$200	$197,850.98
	500	494,627.45
	1,000	989,254.98

If This Is True, *Why Should Anyone Keep Any Money in the Bank?*

Remember, banks are insured and safe—money market funds
are neither. Remember, also, your broker isn't interested
in—or very good at—moving small amounts of savings dollars
around for you. He wants big amounts and few transactions. But
more important, remember this: short-term money market
interest rates have fluctuated widely over time. There are
periods when the rates paid on these "instruments" are lower
than the rates paid by credit unions or savings banks on daily
interest accounts. Treasury Bills, for example, don't always pay
more than passbook savings accounts. Your cash should be

9

working at the best possible rate and at times that rate might be received in the bank. *Don't assume that the more sophisticated an investment sounds the better it is.* There are times when passbook rates can't be topped by money market instruments. When such a time exists, move even your serious savings dollars back to the savings institutions.

If You Can Earn Higher Interest
Should You Cash in Your Savings Certificate?

Under the banking rules that existed before July 1979, it almost always did not make sense to liquidate your certificate of deposit (C.D.) early. The new rules call for a much lighter penalty, so switching may be in your best interest. The minimum penalty for early withdrawal of money from a savings certificate of one year or less now, is the loss of three months' interest. For certificates of over a year, the penalty is the loss of six months' interest.

Although this rule doesn't apply to savings certificates purchased before July 1979, many banks and savings and loan institutions interpret the rule leniently and allow the old certificates to fall under the new rule if money is added to the old certificates. With this allowance, it is possible to add as little as one dollar to your existing savings certificate and qualify for the lesser penalty imposed by the new rule.

If your bank isn't this lenient, these guidelines generally apply. If the C.D. is less than half old, it probably makes sense to change. If it is over half, it probably doesn't. The closer a certificate is to maturity, the higher the new interest rate need be for you to sensibly abandon the old C.D.

Remember, the amount of new interest must exceed the amount of old interest plus penalty, less any tax savings which result. Keep in mind that *the amount of any penalty charged is tax deductible.*

The penalty under the old rule amounts to a reduction of the interest paid to no more than the passbook savings rate less three months' interest at that rate. The penalty calculation is

INVESTMENT	MATURITY	MINIMUM INVESTMENT	HOW OR WHERE TO BUY	UNIQUE FEATURES
Savings account	none	usually none	saving banks, credit unions, savings and loan institutions	Some pay interest from first of month on funds deposited by 10th day.
Money market funds	no restriction	$1,000 to $5,000	directly through fund or through a stockbroker	Interest compounded daily also changes daily.
Savings certificates	6 months to 8 years	$5,000 to $10,000	savings banks, credit unions, savings and loan institutions	penalty for early withdrawal
Treasury Bills	3 months to 12 months	$10,000	directly through Federal Reserve, commercial banks, or stockbrokers	Interest earned is difference between purchase price and face value paid at maturity.
U.S. Agency and short-term notes	3 months or longer	$5,000 to $10,000	directly through Federal Reserve, commercial banks, or stockbrokers	usually ½ percent higher than Treasury obligations
Project notes (tax-exempt)	3 months to 1 year	$5,000 to $25,000	commercial banks or stockbrokers	federal income tax free can be state tax free
Municipal notes	1 month to 1 year	$5,000 to $25,000	commercial banks or stockbrokers	can be both federal and state income tax free
Commercial paper	1 month 9 months	$25,000	commercial banks or stockbrokers	issued by private corporations
Unit trust saving certificate	6 months	$1,000	stockbrokers	marketable

much simpler for a new C.D. Simply take the total amount of interest you will receive by sticking with your C.D. per year and multiply it times the number of years the C.D. will exist. Compare that number to the total amount of interest your replacement investment will earn over the same period. Subtract from the interest to be received from the replacement investment the amount of the penalty. Add back any tax savings that will result from the penalty loss. Compare the old and the new. Chose the investment with the biggest net number.

You can escape all penalties if:

1. you die (no penalty for terminating upon the death of the owner)
2. you become demented (no penalty if the owner is found to be mentally incompetent)
3. you reach fifty-nine-and-a-half years old and the C.D. is in an Individual Retirement Account (IRA) or Keogh account (both are retirement plans).

Unit Trust Six-Month Savings Certificates

The key disadvantage of traditional bank and savings and loan savings certificates is their illiquidity without loss of interest. Another is their $10,000 minimum investment requirement. To overcome these disadvantages many brokerage firms have designed a unit trust made up of six–month certificates of deposits from savings institutions. These C.D. units are available to you in any multiple of $1,000. They can be sold at any time without any interest penalty. Because the units are part of a package of many multimillion-dollar C.D.'s the rate of interest they pay is usually higher than the ones you can get with the same amount of money from your local savings institution. While there isn't any interest penalty for early sale, the basic $1,000 price of the unit may fluctuate. Therefore, if interest rates rise sharply after you make your purchase you could suffer a loss of principal by selling out before maturity. You could also realize a gain if interest rates decline after you make your purchase. Units of C.D.'s are not FDIC or FSLIC insured.

How to Buy the Most for Your Money

As an investor you can usually buy the most money with your money with the highest degree of certainty in the fixed income market. The securities that make up this market are those that promise to pay you a fixed (unchanging) amount of income on specified dates until they mature. Assuming the company remains financially healthy, at maturity they will be redeemed for their face value.

The fixed income market is made up of long-term, intermediate-term, and short-term securities. "Term" has to do with the time until the security matures.

Interest Rates Are Cyclical

Interest rates have historically moved in cycles. While over the years they have climbed significantly, the ascent has not been uninterrupted by major interest rate declines. If you purchase longer term fixed income securities when the rate of interest offered is high, you will probably see the prices of your securities increase when interest rates drop in one of these cycles. In some cases, those gains can be dramatic. More important to many people who choose to invest in longer term, high yield securities is that they are able to continue receiving a high rate of interest even though the prevailing rates have dropped to a much lower level. If you don't "lock in" the high rates but continue to roll over your short term investments, you will probably see the interest rate paid on your money drop below that offered on passbook savings accounts at banks or credit unions when the prevailing interest rates cycle downward.

So, should you buy long-term rather than short-term securities? The question becomes one of investment requirements. If you need liquidity (easy access without penalty), you should use the short-term money market tools such as Treasury Bills or short-term certificates of deposit. If you must maximize the income from your savings and don't foresee a need to dip into your savings program, you should select some longer term fixed income investments. There are people who save more money than they ever plan to spend. If that money is simply accumulating at the low bank passbook interest rate, it makes much more sense to invest those funds in higher yielding long-term fixed income securities.

What Are Fixed Income Securities?

All types of bonds, notes, certificates of deposit, preferred and preference stock are referred to as fixed income investments. They are meant to provide a steady flow of income for your investment rather than any opportunity for growth. Their yields are usually considerably higher than can be obtained with common stocks.

Each security has its own characteristics. Each represents some different relationship to the company that issues it. The most senior security is called a *bond*. A bond is a written promise by the company that issues it to repay this amount of money borrowed on a specified date. In this respect a bond is very much like a home mortgage. In fact, many bonds are first mortgages on the property owned by the company. A bond is also a promise to pay a certain amount of interest every year—either fixed or fluctuating—until it matures and the principal is repaid. Generally, the interest is paid in equal installments twice a year—on the anniversary date of the bond and six months from that date. These interest payments usually arrive as checks in the mail. Bonds are commonly issued, and later bought and sold in $1,000 denominations. Although, when they are first issued, they may be available only in blocks of five for $5,000. A complete listing of bonds can be found in the monthly *Standard and Poor's Register* or *Moody's Bond Record*. Either can be obtained from your broker. Less complete corporate bond listings can be found in the financial section of major newspapers. Those listings include only those bonds that trade on the New York Bond Exchange (not all corporate bonds will) and even those are listed in the newspaper only when a trade occurs in that particular bond on the previous business day.

Once a bond is issued, it can pass through many hands before it finally is repaid (matures) by the original issuer. This is because, like a common stock, a bond is negotiable. It can be bought and sold. While its face value will never vary, its market value will be higher or lower than its face value based on two factors. These are: the *prevailing interest rate* of similar bonds and the *financial condition* of the company. Of these two factors, the easiest to understand is the financial condition. It is like an individual's credit standing. A debt is only as good as the debtor's ability to pay interest and repay principal. Assuming the issuer of the bonds remains a solid, on-going business when the bond's maturity date is reached, the investor will get his money back. However, if the issuer were to go bankrupt in the meantime, then getting money back would be more difficult and the security behind the debt would become important. The lesson to be learned: lend your money only to those firms you believe will be able to repay you. Because investors need guidance in this respect, there exist bond rating services. The most widely respected of these services are Moody's Investor Service, Inc., and Standard and Poor's Corporation. These services continually evaluate the credit worthiness of corporations and assign ratings to their bonds. The ratings represent an assessment of the corporation's ability to pay interest and eventually redeem the bond.

The ratings from top to bottom are:

MOODY'S	S AND P	QUALITY
Aaa	AAA	Highest quality
Aa	AA (±)	Excellent quality
A	A (±)	Good quality
Baa	BBB (±)	Acceptable quality

Ratings go beyond the financial condition of the company. The management of the company is important and so is the environment in which the company does its business. Quality ratings go below the ones listed, but the lower the rating the greater the risk to the investor. Most investors would be best served by bonds that are rated in one of the above categories.

The better quality a corporation, or the smaller debt it has, the higher its rating, and the lesser rate of interest that corporation will have to pay to borrow money. Credit worthiness and amount of acceptable debt will vary by industry. A good general rule to remember is that the better the rating, the lower the risk and the lower the rate of interest an investor will be paid. An unusually high interest rate which is out of line with the interest rates generally available from other bonds should be a red flag. No company will pay a higher rate of interest than it has to to borrow money. In the bond market, as in every other market, you get what you pay for.

For individuals who invest in good quality bonds, a more likely factor to affect the market value of their bonds is the prevailing interest rates of similar new bonds. Interest rates change continually because money is a commodity like any other. Sometimes there is plenty of money available in the economy and sometimes it is very difficult to obtain. Many factors influence the economy's money supply, but the result is the *cost of money*, which is also referred to as the *prevailing interest rate*. If the bond is issued when the economy is flush with money, the rate of interest the company would have to pay to borrow money would be relatively low. As an example, let us assume that the rate of interest a company would have to pay to borrow money is 10 percent, or $100 per $1,000, per year. The company will pay 10 percent interest because that is the prevailing cost of money for corporations of its quality at that time. The 10 percent cost is established by the law of supply and demand. In our illustration let us assume that one year has passed and the supply and demand ratio has changed somewhat. There is less money in the economy and its cost is slightly higher. Rather than costing 10 percent to obtain money, the borrowing company is forced to pay 11 percent to borrow more money with its new bonds. What do you suppose the resale value of the older 10 percent bonds would be? Remember that $1,000 invested in a new bond will bring a return of 11 percent, or $110, per year. Last Year's $1,000 bonds pay 10 percent, or $100, per year. To adjust for the price of the new bonds and the 11 percent prevailing interest rate, the old bonds will have to be priced below $1,000 so that $100 divided by X (the new value of the 10 percent bond) will equal approximately 11 percent, which is the prevailing interest rate. Computed in this manner the 11 percent would be called the bond's *current yield*.

What if the prevailing interest rate were 7 percent rather than 11 percent? Using the same equation, $100 divided by X equals the prevailing interest rate of 7 percent, X would equal an amount greater than the $1,000 face value (see chart).

It is fair to say that at some time in the life of any bond, the bond will sell at a price equal to its face value, below its face value, and above its face value because of the ever-fluctuating interest rates in the economy.

Since the prevailing interest rate changes from day to day and generally moves up and down in cycles, a bond's price will fluctuate above and below its original issue price throughout its life. At maturity it will be redeemed at its face value. Keep in

THE JOURNEY OF OUR BOND THROUGH THE
BOND MARKET FROM ISSUE DATE TO MATURITY

	If the prevailing interest rate is	*The market price of our bond will be*	*Even though the maturity value will always be*
	7%	above face value	$1,000
Our $1,000 10% Bond	10	face value	$1,000
	11	below face value	$1,000

mind that other influences, including a change of credit rating, will also affect the price of the bond.

What this means to an investor is that bonds are usually a better long-term than short-term investment. *Don't put yourself in the position of having to sell your bonds when the market price is below its issue price. Invest only the money you won't need to use in the near term in bonds with lengthy maturity dates.*

Understanding Yield to Maturity

When you buy money there is another term that is used to describe rate of return in addition to current yield. It is called *yield to maturity*. This means that you can measure both the current return and the gain or loss that will be realized by holding the bond to its maturity date.

If you purchased the 10 percent bond, described earlier, when it is selling below its face value (at a discount), you know that by holding it until maturity you will be able to redeem it for

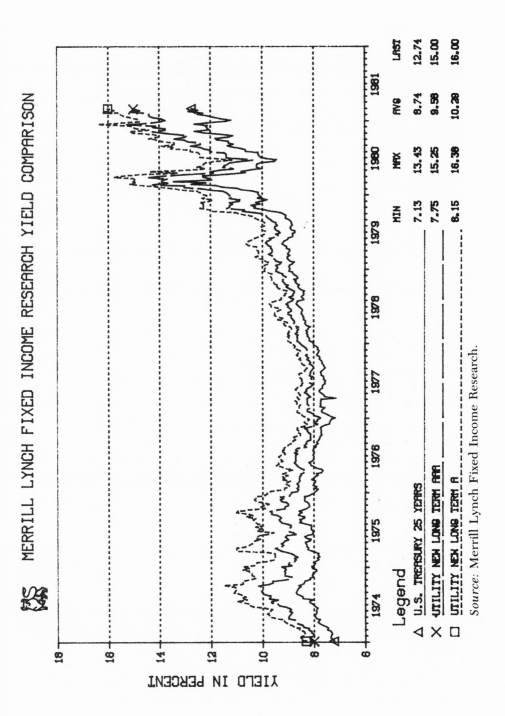

MERRILL LYNCH FIXED INCOME RESEARCH YIELD COMPARISON

YIELD IN PERCENT

		MIN	MAX	AVG	LAST
△	U.S. TREASURY 25 YEARS	7.13	13.43	8.74	12.74
✕	UTILITY NEW LONG TERM AAA	7.75	15.25	9.58	15.00
☐	UTILITY NEW LONG TERM A	8.15	16.38	10.28	16.00

Legend

Source: Merrill Lynch Fixed Income Research.

19

$1,000. The gain you will realize when the bond appreciates from its discounted price to its face value, as well as the interest that the bond pays, are both considered investment return.

Conversely, if you purchased the 10 percent bond at a price above its face value (at a premium), you know that at maturity the bond will be redeemed at face value and you will lose any amount you paid over $1,000 for the bond.

The calculation that takes the gain or loss as well as interest earned into account is made this way. The bond in this example pays 9 percent and will mature in ten years.

	DISCOUNT BOND	PREMIUM BOND
1. Take the face value of the bond and subtract from it the bond's current market price.	$1,000 −920 ――― 80	$1,000 Face Value −1,040 Market Price ――― −40
2. Divide the discount or premium by the years to go before maturity to get the discount or premium per year.	80 ÷ 10 = $8	−40 ÷ 10 = −$4
3. Add one year's interest to get the total annual return.	$90 +8 ――― $98	$90 −4 ――― $86
4. Divide the total return per year by the current price of the bond.	98 ÷ 920 = 10.65%	86 ÷ 1040 = 8.27%
5. Divide the total return per year by the face value of the bond less the discount per year or less the negative premium (plus the premium) per year.	98 ÷ (1000 − 8) = 9.87%	86 ÷ $1000 − (−4), or 86 ÷ (1000 + 4) = 8.56%

	DISCOUNT BOND	PREMIUM BOND
6. Average the answers	10.65	8.27
to 4 and 5 and you	+9.87	+8.56
have computed *yield*	20.52	16.83
to maturity.	÷ 2 =	÷ 2 =
	10.26%	8.415%

You can use this method to find the yield to maturity of any bond listed in the bond table of your newspaper.

The yield given in your daily newspaper is the current yield rather than yield to maturity. For most investors the current yield is a more important number than yield to maturity as it represents money you can spend now. For example, you purchase a bond selling at $800 which pays $80 a year in interest. The current yield is 80/800 or 10 percent. That means that the money you invest in that bond buys 10 percent interest for you, which is paid to you every year in which you own that bond. The fact that the bond will be worth $1,000 at maturity and you will gain an additional $200 is nice to know, and that is why the yield to maturity calculation exists, but remember that you won't be able to spend that extra $200 until the bond matures.

How to Determine Your Strategy About Yield to Maturity

There are logical reasons why you should consider buying bonds at a discount or premium. Among them are: funding your retirement, your children's education, or even providing funds for speculation.

PROVIDING FUNDS FOR RETIREMENT

If you know you are going to retire in seven years you might choose to buy deeply discounted bonds that will mature in seven years. By doing this, you will insure that your capital will be available to you when you need it at retirement. You won't have to worry about what the market price of your bond will be at that time. And even if you have to settle for a lesser rate of current return while you hold the bonds, you may not want a high current return while you are working and in a higher tax bracket than you will be after retirement. This appreciation of the bonds from the discounted price to face value will be more favorably taxed because it is considered a *capital gain* rather than ordinary income. Interest income is taxed as ordinary income in the year in which it is received. Let's put this in real life terms. You are seven years away from retirement and have $10,000 to invest. Your broker shows you these alternatives:

1. ten bonds maturing in twenty years, selling at face value (par), yielding 14 percent interest
2. ten bonds maturing in seven years, selling at face value (par), yielding 10 percent interest
3. fourteen bonds maturing in seven years, selling at $700 each, with a coupon rate of interest of 4 1/2 percent, and a current return of 6.43 percent.

While the highest yielding bond in alternative 1 may appear to be the most attractive choice, it could be the most disastrous. Because when you retire in seven years and need your $10,000, the market price of the bonds could be substantially below face value. On the other hand, that price could be substantially higher.

But when you buy a twenty-year bond with the expectation that you will have to sell it in seven years, you are gambling on how high the prevailing interest rates will be in seven years. And whenever you gamble you stand a chance of losing.

Alternative 2 seems like a reasonable choice. It pays an attractive rate of interest and matures just when you need it.

But the yield to maturity strategy may make alternative *c* the best choice for you. You see, while you work, your tax bracket is probably going to be higher than after you retire. So some part of the 10 percent return you would receive by selecting alternative *b* will be reduced by income taxes. Remember interest income is taxed as ordinary income in the same way as the income from your employment.

Alternative 3 will provide a lesser amount of interest income to be taxed. The major part of your gain is growth of capital. Fourteen bonds were purchased at $700 each. Total investment was $9,800. The value at maturity in seven years will be $14,000.

Long-term capital gains are currently more favorably taxed than ordinary income. Currently 60 percent of the long-term gain (those gains realized in a holding period longer than one year) is excused. Only the remaining 40 percent of the long-term gain is taxed, and that is taxed as ordinary income in the year it is received. If you receive it after you have retired and your income has dropped, the tax will probably be lower than had you received this money in any other way. Even if you are in the 50 percent tax bracket (joint return taxable income in the $60,000 range), the net result of the investment is attractive. The total capital gain will be $14,000 minus $9,800 equals $4,200. Sixty percent or $2,520 is excused from tax. Only $1,680 is subject to tax. At 50 percent the tax would be $840 on the $4,200 gain. In lower tax brackets that amount would be less. In higher brackets the amount would be greater. The point is that long-term *capital gains are better than ordinary income* under our current tax laws.

PROVIDING FUNDS FOR EDUCATION

Purchasing discounted bonds that mature in the years you need money to pay for your children's education is also a sensible idea. You can stagger the maturity dates so that money is available over a number of years. Bonds that mature at a $1,000 face value might be purchased ten or more years before maturity at 30 percent to 50 percent discounts from their face values. This can be an attractive price for a young family struggling to finance a college tuition savings program.

Let's assume that you have two children or grandchildren. One will begin college in ten years, the other in twelve years.

You have $3,000 to invest for each for their college education now. For the oldest child buy a bond which will mature in ten years, another in eleven years, and another in twelve years and so on. For the second child buy bonds that will mature beginning in twelve years. By doing this you will insure that money is available in increments as the student progresses through the years of college. The $3,000 may buy as many as six $1,000 bonds. Accumulate the current interest in a savings account and as it, plus other money, adds up to enough to buy more discounted bonds, add to the education bond portfolio. Chapter 5 will give you some suggestions about how to build this portfolio while taking maximum advantage of the tax laws.

PROVIDING FUNDS FOR SPECULATION

In later sections of this book we will explore investments that are generally considered speculative and which, despite their merit in the minds of many investors, rank as an investment possibility somewhere after the deed to the Brooklyn Bridge and the franchise for suntanning centers on the Equator. But what if some of your hard-earned money became available so that you could take a flyer. It could by using discount bonds.

Buy twenty discounted bonds that mature at retirement time at face value. Pay $15,000 for the twenty bonds. Invest $5,000 in the speculative program. If the worst happens and you lose every dollar you invested, at retirement you will still have $20,000, because the twenty bonds you bought for $15,000 will mature at face value. If the speculative investment is successful, you will have the $20,000 from the bond investment plus whatever that investment returns.

This strategy allows you to "free up" dollars you don't believe you have to invest in something you may not otherwise try.

Or Don't Speculate Invest the entire $20,000 in discounted bonds. If $15,000 will buy twenty bonds, $20,000 will buy twenty-six bonds. At retirement, you are certain of having $26,000 plus interest.

24

Should You Buy Bonds at a Premium?

Traditionally, banks are the biggest buyers of premium bonds. They do it for the extra high current income a premium bond will generate. If you believe that inflation destroys the purchasing power of your dollars, then high current income from your bond purchases should be your goal. The dollars that you will lose when the bonds drop in price from the premium price you paid to the face value you will receive at maturity are worth less and less each year anyway. The higher current return will allow you to reinvest more money *now* to buy money rather than later.

Inflation—A Reason Not to Own Bonds

In recent years the continuing rate of high inflation is an argument against buying money with long-term bonds. Inflation erodes the buying power of money. So both the *interest* that you earn from investing in bonds and the *principal* returned a number of years later when your bond matures at face value, is worth less, in terms of purchasing power, than what your money was worth when you used it to make your original investment.

Therefore, while you can see that buying money with bonds makes more sense than buying money with lesser yielding passbook savings accounts or savings certificates, you should remember that bonds are not the most prudent place to store *all* of your money in times of high inflation.

Types of Bonds

The type of bond a corporation offers also makes a difference in the rate of interest paid and the quality rating of the bond. Some are *mortgage bonds*. These are secured by a specific property that the corporation owns in the same way a house mortgage is secured by a home. The guarantee to the purchaser of a mortgage-backed bond is that, if the corporation becomes unable to make the interest payment as required, the property can be sold to pay the bond holder. Another type of mortgage bond is an *equipment trust certificate.* This type of bond is usually issued by a railroad to purchase railroad cars. The bond holder actually has a lien on specific railroad cars as security for his investment. Generally, these bonds are more secure than *debentures,* which are backed by the "promise" of a corporation to pay. Debentures are similar to signature loans in which the corporation's good name and reputation are the security behind these obligations. There are also bonds known as *subordinated debentures,* which are also promises to pay the bond holder, but are ranked below the company's debentures, the interest on which must be paid before any is paid to subordinated debenture owners. The ranking of bonds in pecking order is academic if you are dealing with the bonds of a high quality corporation but can be very important when you are investing in a financially shaky organization.

One special type of bond, which is really more of a mixed breed—part bond, part common stock—is called a *convertible bond.* In the bond table of your newspaper it is identified with the notation "CV." You might find that this type of security can be a good substitute for common stock because its rate of interest is fixed, unlike the common stock dividend, which can fluctuate. The rate of interest paid by the convertible bond is usually higher than the dividend paid by the common stock. Also, because it is a bond, interest must be paid before any dividend is paid on the common stock. In these respects, it is safer than common stock. It is a substitute for common stock because it is convertible into common stock at a fixed price at the option of the owner. As an example, a convertible bond issued at $1,000 can be converted into fifty shares of common stock at any time at $20 a share. If the common stock sold at $18 a share, the convertible feature would, theoretically, be worthless. But, if the common stock moved up to $25 a share, that feature would make the bond worth $250 more than its face value: $25 minus $20 equals $5 multiplied by fifty shares equals $250.

These advantages make owning a convertible bond a very

attractive investment. Not only will you earn a higher rate of return on your money than if it were invested in the common stock of the same corporation, but you will benefit if the common stock moves up in price. Its principal disadvantages are that a convertible bond generally pays a lower rate of interest than other bonds issued by the same corporation. Also it ranks lower than any other bond of the corporation in respect to its owner's claim on company assets should the company go bust. When originally issued, the conversion price is usually fixed about 15 percent above the market price of the common stock at that time. Therefore, there must be a significant increase in the price of the common stock before the convertibility feature contributes to the value of your bond.

How You Should Buy Bonds

When you buy a bond, you pay a commission to your broker. The amount of your commission is based on the number of bonds you buy and from whom you buy them. It is possible to pay as much as $30 to $50 to purchase a single bond. If you shop around, you may pay only $1.25. Ask your broker about fees before you place your order. Be especially careful if the bond he offers to you is at a "net" price, that is, commission included. You won't have any idea what the commission is unless you ask two or three different brokerage firms the price for the same bond. So ask! One firm may offer the bond at $950 net, another at $920 net. The difference in price is the hidden brokerage commission.

Fixed Returns Are Available to Stock Investors

Besides buying bonds, you can guarantee yourself a fixed return by investing in *preferred stocks*. These stocks are usually issued in $10, $25, $50, and $100 multiples, versus $1,000 for bonds. They can be attractive as investments for three other reasons as well. They pay dividends quarterly rather than semiannually as do bonds. Preferred stocks will nearly always yield more than the common stock of the same company, and the dividend on the preferred must be paid before any common stock owners are paid their dividends.

The disadvantage is that straight preferred stock dividends cannot be raised, unlike common stock dividends. This is the major weakness of all fixed income securities.

There are a few other facts you should know about preferred stocks. *Cumulative preferred stocks* provide that, if for any reason that corporation can't pay the dividend when it is due, the corporation must make up the accumulated dividends before the common stock owners receive any. Nearly all new preferred stock is cumulative. *Participating preferred stock* allows its owners to receive a share of the profits when the company has a particularly good year. This sort of preferred is very rare. *Convertible preferred stock* works like convertible bonds. It allows the preferred stock to be converted into a certain number of common stock shares. This stock will generally offer a lower dividend than regular preferred stock and, of course, will trade more like a common stock. Its price will fluctuate with the fate of the company—up in good times and down in bad. In some cases there are *sinking funds* which allow the company to buy back a certain number of preferred stock shares each year. A sinking fund is simply a pot of money the company uses to repurchase bonds or preferred stock in the market at discount prices as interest rates rise. Stock originally issued at $25 and bought back at $20 is a cheap way for companies to retire debt.

A corporation issues preferred stock because preferred stock doesn't affect the company's bond debt coverage ratio. That is, as far as accountants are concerned, it doesn't count as debt even though it is close in characteristics. Secondly, preferred stock is offered because a corporation finds there is a large market, both corporate and individual, for this type of security. Furthermore, certain tax advantages exist for corporate preferred stock buyers. The dividend is 85 percent tax free on any preferred stock issued after 1956, which is called "new money preferred."

Every time a corporation issues a preferred stock, it sells a different issue with its own rate of interest and price. So, it isn't unusual to find that a corporation has several preferred stock issues, each of which is designated by an alphabetical letter. Preferred "A" would be the oldest. The other series would follow in turn.

Companies can sell one other type of stock that ranks below all of the preferred stock issues but still ahead of the common stock in the quality pecking order. This is called *preference stock*. As the subordinated debenture is to a debenture, preference stock is to preferred. It is a junior obligation that has all of the characteristics of a preferred stock but is subordinate to the preferred stock in the call on corporate dividends and assets. For these reasons, it will pay a slightly higher dividend than preferred stock. Remember, the rule is the lower the quality the higher the yield—and the lower the quality the greater the risk to you the investor.

Bonds and preferred stock usually have what is known as a *call feature*. This allows the corporation to repurchase the issue at a set price, usually above the original issue price, at its discretion. Most call features can't be exercised until the issue is at least five years old, in many instances ten years old. The reason for this is to allow a corporation, which may have had to raise money at an extremely high rate of interest or dividend, the opportunity to rid itself of that debt if interest rates come down. When the preferred stock is called it is usually done at a higher price than when it was originally sold. So that is some compensation to you for losing a high interest bearing security. If a preferred stock or bond is non-callable the abbreviation "n/c" will be used to identify it.

Floating Rates—A Method of Staying Even with Changing Interest Rates

In periods of rising interest rates many investors are reluctant to buy fixed income securities as they fear that continued interest rate rises will depress the value of their purchase. So many bond issuers offer floating rate notes which can eliminate the reason for that fear.

A floating rate note is a bond that pays a fixed rate of interest usually for six months only. After the six-month period is over, the rate is changed to conform to whatever the prevailing interest rate is at the time. Usually, some bench mark such as the prime rate or the Treasury Bill rate is used on which to base the rate for the upcoming six-month period. The higher it is, the higher the rate of interest the floating rate note will pay you.

The main advantages to you are that as a floating rate note owner you are always earning a rate of interest which is close to the prevailing rate in the economy, and because of that the market price of your floating rate note shouldn't wander far from what you paid for it. A $1,000 bond should always sell close to $1,000. Many floating rate issues have another feature that assures your market value will always be close to the face value. That feature is called a *put*. It allows you to "put" the bond (return it without a fee) to the issuer at face value usually once every six months. Floating rate notes without the put provision tend to fluctuate in market value more. They may sell well below face value if the interest rate is adjusted and then interest rates escalate rapidly, leaving you with a comparatively low rate of interest. Some of the notes are convertible into a bond with a fixed rate of return. This allows you to latch onto a guaranteed rate of interest if the floating rate falls to some point below the guaranteed fixed rate.

Bond Funds and Unit Trusts

An easy way to add bonds to your investment mix while perhaps avoiding some of the mysteries of the bond market is to buy money with a bond fund or bond unit trust. Both are portfolios of a large number of bonds. Bond funds are managed by an investment company and the bonds are bought and sold by the fund manager in an effort to earn capital gains as well as interest.

Bond unit trusts are unmanaged and, therefore, unchanging pools of various bonds. Because the bonds in a unit trust portfolio are always the same, the rate of interest it pays will not change. Both can be bought in relatively small dollar amounts —usually $1,000. There are a variety of kinds of bond funds and unit trusts with different objectives and fees.

There are "intermediate" term (ten years or less) trusts, tax free and corporate bond trusts, certificate of deposit unit trusts, and trusts of U.S. government bonds—heavily weighted with "Ginnie Maes" (bonds from the Government National Mortgage Association). Interest is usually paid monthly or can be reinvested in an "investment accumulation program," which is a mutual fund of the same type of securities.

The unit trusts and bond funds can be sold at any time but will vary in price like any fixed income security.

The commission you will pay to buy a unit trust will be between 1/2 of 1 percent to 5 1/2 percent depending on which company sponsors the trust and its length of maturity. Bond funds are available without any sales fee (no load), and through brokerage firms for as much as 8 percent commission. There are no fees involved in selling either. Because unit trusts are unmanaged, they charge no management fee. Bond funds, which are managed, charge an annual fee that is usually around 1/2 of 1 percent.

How to Buy U.S. Government Money

Someone once said that it takes a big dog to weigh five hundred pounds. It also takes a big government to owe many trillion dollars. Because that debt exists and is ever-growing, there are a host of ways to buy money from Uncle Sam. You can buy it for very short or very long periods of time. You can buy U.S. government guaranteed money which is tax free, partially tax free, or tax deferred. It is possible as well to buy money that is paid to you monthly, semiannually, or even the day you make your purchase. In short, Uncle Sam's insatiable appetite for funds has given birth to a range of securities as diverse as Tennessee Valley Authority bonds and the Robert F. Kennedy Stadium bonds. The TVA bonds are traded like those of major corporations on the New York Bond Exchange and the R.F.K. Stadium bonds are traded like those of cities and states in the municipal bond market.

The U.S. Government securities that are most widely used by individual investors to buy money from Uncle Sam are listed below. Each of these is in some way backed by the federal government or one of its agencies. They have been categorized according to the income tax advantage they offer.

1. Federal Securities that Pay Tax Deferred Money
   Savings Bonds
   Series E and EE
   Series H and HH
2. Federal Securities that Pay Money Exempt from Federal
   Income Tax
   > Public Housing Authority Notes and Bonds
3. Federal Securities that Pay Money Exempt from State
   and Local Income Taxes
   > U.S. Treasury Bills, Notes, and Bonds
   > Farm Credit System Notes and Bonds
   > Federal Land Banks
   > Federal Intermediate Credit Banks
   > Federal Farm Credit Banks
   > Banks for Cooperatives
   > Federal Home Loan Bank Notes and Bonds
   > Government National Mortgage Association Certificates
   > U.S. Postal Service Bonds
   > Washington Metropolitan Area Transit Authority Bonds
   > General Service Administration Bonds
   > Tennessee Valley Authority Bonds
4. Federal Securities that Have No Tax Advantage
   > Federal National Mortgage Association Notes and Bonds
   > Maritime Administration Bonds

The Most Widely Held
U.S. Government Securities

When most people think of U.S. government bonds they think of savings bonds. These are the Series E, Series EE, Series H, and Series HH bonds. Series E and Series H bonds are being phased out and can no longer be purchased. Series EE bonds can be obtained in relatively small dollar amounts: $50, $75, $100, $200, $500, and larger amounts: $1,000, $5,000, and $10,000. The maximum purchase per individual is $15,000 in any one year. They are purchased at a *discount*, that is, 50 percent of their face value. At maturity, they are worth *par*, face value. They mature in nine years. That growth in value works out to a 7 1/2 percent rate of interest per year.

While Series EE bonds are generally miserable investments for most people because of the low rate of interest they pay, they can be an attractive investment for certain individuals for two reasons. The first is that a Series EE bond investment can be done painlessly through a payroll savings plan or at any bank. Buying these bonds can be a good forced savings program. The second reason is that the money you buy with Series EE bonds is tax deferred. That is, you don't have to pay any income tax on the interest until the bonds mature. This is a distinct advantage if you expect to be in a lower income tax bracket when that happens.

Unfortunately, that is rarely the case. Most Series E and Series EE bond buyers are frugal people who, over the years, do such a good job with their savings and investing programs that they never drop into a lower tax bracket. For these people, maturation dates can be painfully taxing—since the entire amount of money bought is treated by the IRS as ordinary income. It is heaped on top of your other taxable income and subjected to the full force of your high tax bracket. The only way to avoid the tax bite is to exchange the Series E or Series EE bonds for Series HH bonds. This is considered a tax-free exchange. Series HH bonds *pay* interest rather than *accrue* interest. While the interest from Series HH bonds is taxable in the year it is paid, the Series HH bonds do at least provide a way of deferring the tax bite on the interest built up over the years on Series E or Series EE bonds. They also provide current interest payments at the rate of 7 1/2 percent, which can be used by the investor in the year in which it is earned.

RATES OF INTEREST CAN IMPROVE

The president has the authority to raise rates by as much as one percentage point during a six-month period to keep the savings bond market somewhat competitive with other investments.

The Treasury Bill Mystique

After savings bonds, the most widely used and certainly most widely discussed U.S. government security is the Treasury Bill. "T-Bills," as they are called, are Uncle Sam's shortest term security. They are usually sold with three-, six-, or twelve-month maturities. They are available in $10,000 minimum amounts and additional multiples of $5,000. Like Series EE bonds, they are issued at a discount and mature at face value. The difference between issue price and maturation value is the interest earned.

A new interest rate is set every Monday by competitive bid. Individual investors don't usually submit a bid, as the minimum is 1 million dollars, but accept the rate offered as a result of the average bids of the large institutional investors.

Brokerage houses and banks generally charge a $25 to $30 fee to purchase the T-Bills for you. That fee can materially reduce the net-after-fee return from a T-Bill. The way to beat that is to buy the bill directly from your nearest Federal Reserve Bank or the Treasury by sending a certified check or official bank check for the full amount. The Federal Reserve Bank will return the difference to you after the interest rate has been determined. For example, if you bought a $10,000 three-month T-Bill for $9,800, the Federal Reserve Bank would immediately refund $200 to you. At maturity your entire $10,000 would be returned. You could also use your matured bill to purchase a new one.

TRUE INTEREST FROM A TREASURY BILL

As T-Bills are bought at a discount and the difference between par value and the purchase price is returned to you at the time of purchase, you can actually earn a higher rate of interest than the stated rate. That is because the money returned can be invested to buy even more money. The chart on pages 38 and 39 shows you the yield you will have to earn from a bond or certificate of deposit to beat a lower yielding T-Bill.

For example, if the T-Bill paid a 14 1/2 percent rate of

interest for six months, you would have to earn at least 15.24 percent in a C.D. to equal it.

Remember also that T-Bills are state and local income tax exempt. That also adds to your true return. For an investor whose state and local income taxes are high, the exemption is a decided advantage.

BUYING TREASURY BILLS WITHOUT A FEE

By mailing the following letter to the Federal Reserve Bank nearest you with your certified check for at least $10,000, you will save the fee a stockbroker or commercial bank would charge you.

To: The Federal Reserve Bank
Sirs:

I hereby submit this tender for currently offered U.S. Treasury Bill of the (three-, six-, or twelve-month) maturity. Enclosed you will find my certified check for $10,000. This is a noncompetitive bid. Please send the receipt to me at:

_____

_____

_____

Sincerely,

_____

_____

Note: T-Bills are not registered in the owner's name and they are no longer issued as a certificate. Instead, ownership is in book-entry form with the Federal Reserve.

Treasury Bills can also be purchased from the Bureau of the Public Debt, Department of the Treasury, 15th Street and New York Avenue, NW, Washington, D.C. 20226.

YIELD EQUIVALENT TABLE

DISC.	30 Days		60 Days		90 Days		120 Days	
	EQUIV BD YLD	EQUIV C.D. YLD	EQUIV BD YLD	EQUIV C.D. YLD	EQUIV BD YLD	EQUIV C.D. YLD	EQUIV BD YLD	EQUIV C.D. YLD
13.25	13.58	13.40	13.74	13.55	13.89	13.70	14.05	13.86
13.50	13.84	13.65	14.00	13.81	14.17	13.97	14.33	14.14
13.75	14.10	13.91	14.27	14.07	14.44	14.24	14.61	14.41
14.00	14.36	14.27	14.53	14.33	14.71	14.51	14.89	14.69
14.25	14.62	14.42	14.80	14.60	14.98	14.78	15.17	14.96
14.50	14.88	14.68	15.07	14.86	15.25	15.05	15.45	15.24
14.75	15.14	14.93	15.33	15.12	15.53	15.31	15.73	15.51
15.00	15.40	15.19	15.60	15.38	15.80	15.58	16.01	15.79
15.25	15.66	15.45	15.87	15.65	16.07	15.85	16.29	16.07
15.50	15.92	15.70	16.13	15.91	16.35	16.12	16.57	16.34
15.75	16.18	15.96	16.40	16.17	16.62	16.40	16.85	16.62
16.00	16.44	16.22	16.67	16.44	16.90	16.67	17.14	16.90
16.25	16.70	16.47	16.93	16.70	17.17	16.94	17.42	17.18
16.50	16.96	16.73	17.20	16.97	17.45	17.21	17.70	17.46
16.75	17.22	16.99	17.47	17.23	17.72	17.48	17.99	17.74
17.00	17.48	17.24	17.74	17.50	18.00	17.75	18.27	18.02
17.25	17.74	17.50	18.01	17.76	18.28	18.23	18.56	18.30
17.50	18.01	17.76	18.28	18.03	18.55	18.30	18.84	18.58
17.75	18.27	18.02	18.55	18.29	18.83	18.57	19.13	18.87
18.00	18.53	18.27	18.81	18.56	19.11	18.85	19.41	19.15

150 Days		180 Days		270 Days		360 Days	
EQUIV BD YLD	EQUIV C.D. YLD	EQUIV BD YLD	EQUIV C.D. YLD	EQUIV BD YLD	EQUIV C.D. YLD	EQUIV BD YLD	EQUIV C.D. YLD
14.22	14.02	14.39	14.19	14.57	14.71	14.94	15.27
14.50	14.30	14.68	14.48	14.87	15.02	15.25	15.61
14.79	14.59	14.97	14.71	15.17	15.33	15.57	15.94
15.07	14.87	15.26	15.05	15.47	15.64	15.88	16.28
15.36	15.15	15.56	15.34	15.77	15.96	16.20	16.62
15.65	15.43	15.85	15.63	16.08	16.27	16.52	16.96
15.93	15.72	16.15	15.92	16.38	16.58	16.84	17.30
16.22	16.00	16.44	16.22	16.69	16.90	17.17	17.65
16.51	16.28	16.74	16.51	16.99	17.22	17.49	17.99
16.80	16.57	17.04	16.80	17.30	17.54	17.82	18.34
17.09	16.86	17.33	17.10	17.61	17.86	18.14	18.69
17.38	17.14	17.63	17.39	17.91	18.18	18.47	19.05
17.67	17.43	17.93	17.69	18.22	18.51	18.80	19.40
17.96	17.72	18.23	17.98	18.54	18.83	19.13	19.76
18.26	18.01	18.53	18.28	18.85	19.16	19.47	20.12
18.55	18.30	18.84	18.58	19.16	19.48	19.80	20.48
18.84	18.59	19.14	18.88	19.47	19.81	20.14	20.85
19.14	18.88	19.44	19.18	19.79	20.14	20.47	21.21
19.43	19.17	19.75	19.48	20.11	20.48	20.81	21.58
19.73	19.46	20.05	19.78	20.42	20.81	21.15	21.95

Boundaries of Federal Reserve Districts and their Branch Territories

January 1978

LEGEND

— Boundaries of Federal Reserve Districts

— Boundaries of Federal Reserve Branch Territories

⊛ Board of Governors of the Federal Reserve System

⊙ Federal Reserve Bank Cities

• Federal Reserve Branch Cities

· Federal Reserve Bank Facility

List of Federal Reserve Banks and Branches

Federal Reserve Bank	Address
BOSTON*	600 Atlantic Avenue, Boston, Massachusetts 02106
NEW YORK*	33 Liberty Street (Federal Reserve P.O. Station), New York, New York 10045
Buffalo Branch	160 Delaware Avenue (P.O. Box 961), Buffalo, New York 14240
PHILADELPHIA	100 North Sixth Street (P.O. Box 66), Philadelphia, Pennsylvania 19105
CLEVELAND*	1455 East Sixth Street (P.O. Box 6387), Cleveland, Ohio 44101
Cincinnati Branch	150 East Fourth Street (P.O. Box 999), Cincinnati, Ohio 45201
Pittsburgh Branch	717 Grant Street (P.O. Box 867), Pittsburgh, Pennsylvania 15230
RICHMOND*	701 East Byrd Street (P.O. Box 27622), Richmond, Virginia 23261
Baltimore Branch	114-120 East Lexington Street (P.O. Box 1378), Baltimore, Maryland 21203
Charlotte Branch	401 South Tryon Street (P.O. Box 30248), Charlotte, North Carolina 28230
Culpeper Communications and Records Center	P.O. Drawer 20, Culpeper, Virginia 22701
ATLANTA	104 Marietta Street, NW., Atlanta, Georgia 30303 (P.O. Box 1731, Atlanta, Georgia 30301)
Birmingham Branch	1801 Fifth Avenue, North (P.O. Box 10447), Birmingham, Alabama 35202
Jacksonville Branch	515 Julia Street, Jacksonville, Florida 32231
Miami Branch	3770 S.W. 8th Street, Coral Gables, Florida 33178 (P.O. Box 520847, Miami, Florida)
Nashville Branch	301 Eighth Avenue, North, Nashville, Tennessee 37203
New Orleans Branch	525 St. Charles Avenue (P.O. Box 61630), New Orleans, Louisiana 70161
CHICAGO*	230 South LaSalle Street (P.O. Box 834), Chicago, Illinois 60690
Detroit Branch	160 Fort Street, West (P.O. Box 1059), Detroit, Michigan 48231
ST. LOUIS	411 Locust Street (P.O. Box 442), St. Louis, Missouri 63166
Little Rock Branch	325 West Capitol Avenue (P.O. Box 1261), Little Rock, Arkansas 72203
Louisville Branch	410 South Fifth Street (P.O. Box 32710), Louisville, Kentucky 40232
Memphis Branch	200 North Main Street (P.O. Box 407), Memphis, Tennessee 38101
MINNEAPOLIS	250 Marquette Avenue, Minneapolis, Minnesota 55480
Helena Branch	400 North Park Avenue, Helena, Montana 59601
KANSAS CITY	925 Grand Avenue (Federal Reserve Station), Kansas City, Missouri 64198
Denver Branch	1020 16th Street (P.O. Box 5228, Terminal Annex), Denver, Colorado 80217
Oklahoma City Branch	226 Northwest Third Street (P.O. Box 25129), Oklahoma City, Oklahoma 73125
Omaha Branch	102 South Seventeenth Street, Omaha, Nebraska 68102
DALLAS	400 South Akard Street (Station K), Dallas, Texas 75222
El Paso Branch	301 East Main Street (P.O. Box 100), El Paso, Texas 79999
Houston Branch	1701 San Jacinto Street (P.O. Box 2578), Houston, Texas 77001
San Antonio Branch	126 East Nueva Street (P.O. Box 1471), San Antonio, Texas 78295
SAN FRANCISCO	400 Sansome Street (P.O. Box 7702), San Francisco, California 94120
Los Angeles Branch	409 West Olympic Boulevard (P.O. Box 2077), Los Angeles, California 90051
Portland Branch	915 S.W. Stark Street (P.O. Box 3436), Portland, Oregon 97208
Salt Lake City Branch	120 South State Street (P.O. Box 30780), Salt Lake City, Utah 84125
Seattle Branch	1015 Second Avenue (P.O. Box 3567), Seattle, Washington 98124

*Additional offices of these Banks are located at Lewiston, Maine 04240; Windsor Locks, Connecticut 06096; Cranford, New Jersey 07016; Jericho, New York 11753; Utica Oriskany, New York 13424; Columbus, Ohio 43216; Columbia, South Carolina 29210; Charleston, West Virginia 25311; Des Moines, Iowa 50306; Indianapolis, Indiana 46204; and Milwaukee, Wisconsin 53202.

(8/80)

41

Treasury Notes and Bonds

Treasury Bills, Notes, and Bonds are all guaranteed by the U.S. government and issued directly by the U.S. Treasury. Treasury Notes and Bonds have longer maturities and are more like corporate bonds than Treasury Bills. Treasury Notes mature from one to ten years. Treasury Bonds are issued for periods longer than ten years. They both pay interest semiannually like corporate bonds and are issued at face value rather than at a discount. When first issued, they are usually sold in $5,000 minimum amounts but they can be bought and sold in the secondary market in $1,000 units. Their prices will fluctuate like any other bonds and you can find them listed every day in the *Wall Street Journal* in a separate Treasury Securities section and in many other newspapers. You can't take the price listed in the paper and expect just that for your purchase. There are two reasons for that, which follow:

Government Securities Are Priced Differently The prices quoted in the *Journal* are for *round lots*, which in Uncle Sam's parlance means multiples of $1,000,000. Prices for $1,000 multiples or odd lots, will be somewhat higher to buy and lower to sell. Government securities prices are quoted in points with par equal to one hundred points. Fractions are expressed in 32nds, one of which equals three and one-eighth cents. So, if you see a price of 99.20, it means that a $1,000 face value bond is selling for $996.25.

$$99\ 20/32 = 99\ 10/16 = 99\ 5/8 = 99.625 = \$996.25$$

A value scale of 32nds looks like this:

GOVERNMENT FRACTION	DOLLAR AMOUNT	CORPORATE BOND EQUIVALENT
1/32nd	$0.3125	1/8 point
4/32nd	1.25	1/4 point
8/32nd	2.50	3/8 point
12/32nd	3.75	3/8 point

GOVERNMENT FRACTION	DOLLAR AMOUNT	CORPORATE BOND EQUIVALENT
16/32nd	5.00	1/2 point
20/32nd	6.25	5/8 point
24/32nd	7.50	3/4 point
28/32nd	8.75	7/8 point
32/32nd	10.00	1 point

Mark Up or Mark Down The second reason has to do with the fee the brokerage firm or bank will charge you to buy or sell the government security. It shouldn't cost much to trade a government security, but whatever the commission, expect it to vary based on the length of maturity. The longer the maturity, the higher the charge. The shorter the length of maturity, the lower the charge.

Because most brokerage firms and banks will show you only a "net" price for your purchase which includes the commission, it makes sense to ask how much of a commission is included in the price you are quoted. *A high commission cost will adversely affect the yield.* You must figure the price of the security plus commission to determine the true yield. Therefore, you may wish to give your broker or bank a "limit" order. If you see in the newspaper the security in which you are interested was 98.4 "asked", you know the price was 98 4/32, or $981.25. Since the commission cost should rarely be over $5 per note or bond, you could offer to buy the security for $986.25 "net" or less. This higher price offer will also allow for the "odd lot differential"; the fact that your price will be higher because you are buying less than a $1,000,000 round lot. Make certain at the time you place your order that there are no additional service charges that will be tacked on.

If you buy the U.S. government notes or bonds when they are first issued by the government, you can obtain them without any commission charge. The broker gets paid—but by Uncle Sam rather than by you.

You Can Do Better with "Agencies"

If you like the idea of owning a bond or note issued by Uncle Sam, you can earn higher interest with one of his "agencies" than you can with a Treasury Note or Bond. Bills, bonds, and notes issued directly by the U.S. Treasury are backed by the full faith and credit of the U.S. government. Many other securities are issued by various U.S. government agencies. Each of the agencies was authorized by Congress. While a few of the agency securities have no direct U.S. government backing, most notably those issued by the World Bank and by the Inter-American Development Bank, other securities enjoy varying levels of guarantees. It is as difficult to imagine the federal government allowing one of its agency securities to go into default, as it is to imagine the federal government failing to honor the insurance provided by the Federal Deposit Insurance Corporation (FDIC) or the Federal Savings and Loan Insurance Corporation (FSLIC), both of which are government agencies.

GOVERNMENT AGENCY AND MISCELLANEOUS SECURITIES

FNMA ISSUES

Rate	Mat	Bid	Asked	Yield
9.70	9.83	96.28	97.4	15.01
7.88	10.84	95.6	95.16	15.22
12.22	6.85	97.12	97.28	13.90

FEDERAL FARM CREDIT

Rate	Mat	Bid	Asked	Yield
15.3	7.84	99.23	99.27	15.49
7.2	9.85	90.20	91.4	13.72

FIC BANK DEBS

Rate	Mat	Bid	Asked	Yield
15.8	11.83	100.12	100.20	14.82
11.85	10.85	96.24	97.8	13.68

GOVERNMENT AGENCY AND MISCELLANEOUS SECURITIES

FEDERAL LAND BANK

Rate	Mat	Bid	Asked	Yield
8.70	7.83	89.20	90.4	13.53
7.35	1.97	60.16	62.16	12.97

How to Read the Chart and Choose Between Agency "Look Alikes"

After determining the level of U.S. government backing you require of your investment and its tax status, *yield* and *maturity date* should become the primary criteria for selection. As an investor, you should try to buy the highest yield available for the time you want your money invested. For example, if you are shopping for the highest yield obtainable for two years, look under the column marked "Mat" for those securities of each agency that *mature* in two years. Then look under the column marked "yield" to find the highest yield. You can then compare one agency's two-year yield with another's. Importantly, the yield shown is *yield to maturity* rather than current yield. The highest yield to maturity may not provide as high a level of current income as you are looking for. You can compute current yield by taking the figure listed under "Rate," and dividing it by the figure listed under "Asked." Remember, the actual asked price will probably be higher, as the one quoted in the newspaper is for round lots—that is, $1,000,000 amounts. And, of course, it was yesterday's price. Keep in mind that prices change in the bond market by the minute.

For some investors, including tax-exempt retirement funds and nonprofit associations, the highest yield to maturity is important rather than the highest current yield, as they have no income taxes to worry about. For the rest of the world, the current income is taxed as earned *interest* and, depending on the security, may be state and local income tax free. The difference between purchase price and maturity value is taxed as *capital gain* if the security was bought below face value (par). However, if it was bought above par, the loss at maturity will not be allowed as a capital loss. See below:

SECURITY A		SECURITY B
$970	purchase price	$1,040
$1,000	maturity value	$1,000
+ $30		− $40

Capital gain, short or long term depending on length of time security was held.	Cannot be called a capital loss, as the IRS says you knew it would be worth only $1,000 at maturity when you made your purchase.

BE PREPARED TO PAY IMMEDIATELY

Most government securities have "next day settlements." This means that you are required to pay for the security the day after it is purchased. Some "settle" in five business days and a few others may not "settle" for weeks. Ask at the time of purchase. Remember also that you won't begin earning any interest on your investment until the settlement date.

What Government Bonds Are Used For

The mind-boggling number of U.S. government agency securities that exist reflect the size of the federal government. For the curious taxpayer, as well as investor, the following brief descriptions may be helpful.

Public Housing Authority Bonds Issued by local authorities to finance low-rent housing projects, these bonds are backed by the Federal Housing Assistance Administration and are, therefore, backed by the full faith and credit of Uncle Sam.

Farm Credit System Notes and Bonds Four types of securities exist to extend credit to the American farmer, rancher, and agricultural producer. The Federal Intermediate Credit Bank securities and Banks for Cooperatives provide short- and intermediate-term credit. The Federal Land Bank provides intermediate- and long-term credit. The newer Federal Farm Credit Bank securities will eventually be the only security offered by the Federal Farm Credit System.

Federal Home Loan Bank Securities These securities provide funds for a reserve credit agency for member savings and loan associations and other thrift institutions that make home mortgage loans.

Federal National Mortgage Association Fannie Mae, as it is called, is a government-sponsored corporation, owned entirely by private stockholders to serve as a secondary market for the insured or guaranteed mortgages of the Federal Housing Administration, Veterans Administration, or Farmers Home Administration. The association provides liquidity on mortgage investments by buying mortgages when normal funds are plentiful.

Agency bonds Traded like corporate bonds, these have been issued by specific U.S. government branches: U.S. Postal Service bonds, Washington Metropolitan Area Transit Authority bonds, General Service Administration bonds, and Tennessee Valley Authority bonds.

Two of the most interesting and unique government agency securities are called Ginnie Maes and Flower Bonds.

Ginnie Maes Ginnie Maes are securities issued by the Government National Mortgage Association. They are unique because they pay the investors who own them a *different amount of income every month*. A Ginnie Mae certificate represents a pool of Federal Housing Administration or Veterans Administration home mortgages. As the people who owe the mortgages in the pool make monthly payments, the payments to the investors who own them are also monthly. As part of the mortgage payment is a payoff of principal and part is interest, the amount paid to the investor varies. It also varies because the certificate represents ownership in a very large pool of mortgages consisting of thousands of mortgages. Each month some homeowners sell their homes and pay off their mortgages. Others may pay off their mortgages in other ways or even pay a few months ahead. This causes the amount of payment to the investors to vary. That payment consists of both interest and principal. The return of principal gradually reduces the amount invested and an investor's return is calculated only on dollars remaining invested. Although it is impossible to predict the average life of any specific mortgage pool, the experience of the Federal Housing Administration, after twenty-five-plus years, indicates that the average life of most single-family FHA and VA mortgages is approximately twelve years. Therefore, the Ginnie Mae estimated maturity is twelve years.

Ginnie Mae dealers calculate that because of the monthly cash flow as opposed to the semiannual interest payments from traditional bonds, an investor needs to earn .14 percent more in a traditional bond to equal the return from a Ginnie Mae. For example, if a Ginnie Mae were to yield 8.46 percent, one would need to earn 8.60 percent in another investment to equal the return. This is because it is assumed that the investor will reinvest his monthly interest payments to obtain additional interest income. Ginnie Maes make sense to an investor who likes the idea of a monthly income check from an intermediate-term U.S. government-backed security. Ginnie Maes represent one of Uncle Sam's largest debts and their success has brought into existence other types of similar securities.

The graduated-payment mortgage security was first dubbed "GIPPUM," but after some negative reaction, rechristened "JEEP." JEEPs are pools of mortgages with payments that increase over time as the mortgagee's age and—theoretically—

income, increase. Graduated-payment mortgages make it easier for younger buyers to afford new homes. Payments in the early years are a lot less than the amount that would be necessary to pay all the interest and principal due on a conventional mortgage loan with level monthly payments.

The success of the government-backed securities has encouraged the birth of single-family conventional mortgage pools. These securities, called "Connie Macs," are not guaranteed by Uncle Sam, but are insured by private companies. Some of these pools are made of *variable rate mortgages.* In these the interest rate paid by the homeowner and received by the investor fluctuates with the prevailing rate of interest. It goes up when interest rates rise and down when the rates decline. Because these securities are not backed by the U.S. government, the interest rate they pay is higher than a Ginnie Mae mortgage pool.

If the idea seems appealing but the $25,000 price tag a little steep, brokerage firms offer unit trust pools of Ginnie Mae securities that can be purchased in $1,000 minimum amounts. Unit trusts are described in detail in the Glossary (Chapter 11).

Flower Bonds—A Way to Save Estate Taxes As the horrible thought of your estate tax bill flashes in your mind, it will undoubtedly give you great comfort to know that you can foil the IRS one last time.

Certain Treasury Bonds, you see, can be bought at a substantial discount from their face value and turned in at face value in payment of your estate tax bill. There are fifteen such issues.

A bond purchased at $800 a day before your death would be worth $1,000 the day after, in payment of your estate taxes. It is even possible to buy Flower Bonds with 10 percent margin. Eight thousand dollars could buy $80,000 of bonds, which would become worth $100,000 to the IRS in payment of your estate taxes. A $20,000 return on an $8,000 investment in such a short period is a "healthy return" indeed. The main drawback is that the entire value of the bonds will be counted in the estate for estate tax purposes.

4

How to Buy Tax-Free Money

If you think the cost of housing will be the biggest expense during your lifetime, think again. According to actuarial tables, the average couple that married in 1980 and produced two children will have earnings over a forty-eight-year span that exceed one *million* dollars in terms of 1980 dollars.

The biggest expense you will pay is *taxes*, which will amount to $244,500. Your next biggest expense will be housing with an expenditure of $238,500. Next comes food at $169,500, and then comes transportation at $151,500.

It is easy to see then, that for many people successful earning of a higher rate of taxable interest is not the real answer. In fact, a higher *taxable* interest may compound your problems.

The goal of a successful investor should be to maximize the *after tax* return on savings dollars.

Let's assume you purchase a $10,000 U.S. government bond that buys you 9 percent interest and that you are in the 30 percent tax bracket. Look at the following chart.

$10,000	investment
9%	interest
$ 900	annual earnings before federal income tax
$ 900	income
× 30%	tax bracket
$ 270	federal income tax
$ 900	earnings before federal income tax
− 270	tax
$ 630	after tax earnings

$$\frac{630}{\$10,000} = 6.3\% \text{ after tax return}$$

From this example you can see that the interest you bought with your $10,000 investment was only 6.3 percent after taxes rather than the seemingly high 9 percent. And the higher your tax bracket, the less attractive the 9 percent taxable rate of interest becomes. In the 50 percent tax bracket, the after tax return is only 4.5 percent.

This is why investors who are in the 30 percent tax bracket and higher would, in most cases, be better off with tax-free investments than taxable ones. How do you determine your tax bracket? Take a look at your last year's tax return. The amount of money you report as taxable income after all the deductions and exemptions have been subtracted should be compared to the following table. Your tax bracket depends on whether you are single or married filing your tax return with your spouse. There is a column for each category of taxpayer. Your tax bracket can be found below your taxable income. As you can see, the higher your tax bracket the more sense it makes to use tax-free investments.

You may have heard of the term *tax inflation*. As you look over the table it will become clear how that term affects you. Inflation pushes all our income levels higher. Since costs move higher to keep up with rising incomes, high incomes don't necessarily mean a better standard of living.

Taxable Equivalent Yields

Based on tax rates in effect August 15, 1980.

To see what a taxable security would have to yield to equal the take-home yield of a tax-free bond find your taxable income and read across.

(Income Brackets—$ Thousands)

Single Return	$10.8 to $12.9	$12.9 to $15.0		$15.0 to $18.2		$18.2 to $23.5		$23.5 to $28.8		$28.8 to $34.1	$34.1 to $41.5		$41.5 to $55.3		$55.3 to $81.8		$81.8 to $108.3	over $108.3
Joint Return	$16.0 to $20.2		$20.2 to $24.6		$24.6 to $29.9		$29.9 to $35.2		$35.2 to $45.8		$45.8 to $60.0	$60.0 to $85.6		$85.6 to $109.4		$109.4 to $162.4	$162.4 to $215.4	over $215.4
% Tax Bracket	24%	26%	28%	30%	32%	34%	37%	39%	43%	44%	49%	54%	55%	59%	63%	64%	68%	70%
Tax-Exempt Yield																		
6.00	7.89	8.11	8.33	8.57	8.82	9.09	9.52	9.84	10.53	10.71	11.76	13.04	13.33	14.63	16.22	16.67	18.75	20.00
6.10	8.03	8.24	8.47	8.71	8.97	9.24	9.68	10.00	10.70	10.89	11.96	13.26	13.56	14.88	16.49	16.94	19.06	20.33
6.20	8.16	8.38	8.61	8.86	9.12	9.39	9.84	10.16	10.88	11.07	12.16	13.38	13.78	15.12	16.76	17.22	19.37	20.67
6.25	8.22	8.45	8.68	8.93	9.19	9.47	9.92	10.25	10.96	11.16	12.25	13.59	13.89	15.24	16.89	17.36	19.53	20.83
6.30	8.29	8.51	8.75	9.00	9.26	9.55	10.00	10.33	11.05	11.25	12.35	13.70	14.00	15.37	17.03	17.50	19.69	21.00
6.40	8.42	8.65	8.89	9.14	9.41	9.70	10.16	10.49	11.23	11.43	12.55	13.91	14.22	15.61	17.30	17.78	20.00	21.33
6.50	8.55	8.78	9.03	9.29	9.56	9.85	10.32	10.66	11.40	11.61	12.75	14.13	14.44	15.85	17.57	18.06	20.31	21.67
6.60	8.68	8.92	9.17	9.43	9.71	10.00	10.48	10.82	11.58	11.79	12.94	14.35	14.67	16.10	17.84	18.33	20.63	22.00
6.70	8.82	9.05	9.31	9.57	9.85	10.15	10.63	10.98	11.75	11.96	13.14	14.57	14.89	16.34	18.11	18.61	20.94	22.33
6.75	8.88	9.12	9.37	9.64	9.93	10.23	10.71	11.07	11.84	12.05	13.24	14.67	15.00	16.46	18.24	18.75	21.09	22.50
6.80	8.95	9.19	9.44	9.71	10.00	10.30	10.79	11.15	11.93	12.14	13.33	14.78	15.11	16.59	18.38	18.89	21.25	22.67
6.90	9.08	9.32	9.58	9.86	10.15	10.45	10.95	11.31	12.11	12.32	13.53	15.00	15.33	16.83	18.65	19.17	21.56	23.00
7.00	9.21	9.46	9.72	10.00	10.29	10.61	11.11	11.48	12.28	12.50	13.73	15.22	15.56	17.07	18.92	19.44	21.88	23.33
7.10	9.34	9.59	9.86	10.14	10.44	10.76	11.27	11.64	12.46	12.68	13.92	15.43	15.78	17.32	19.19	19.72	22.19	23.67
7.20	9.47	9.73	10.00	10.29	10.59	10.91	11.43	11.80	12.63	12.86	14.12	15.65	16.00	17.56	19.46	20.00	22.50	24.00
7.25	9.54	9.80	10.07	10.36	10.66	10.98	11.51	11.89	12.72	12.95	14.22	15.76	16.11	17.68	19.59	20.14	22.66	24.17
7.30	9.61	9.86	10.14	10.43	10.74	11.06	11.59	11.97	12.81	13.04	14.31	15.87	16.22	17.80	19.73	20.28	22.81	24.33
7.40	9.74	10.00	10.28	10.57	10.88	11.21	11.75	12.13	12.98	13.21	14.51	16.09	16.44	18.05	20.00	20.56	23.13	24.67
7.50	9.87	10.14	10.42	10.71	11.03	11.36	11.90	12.30	13.16	13.39	14.71	16.30	16.67	18.29	20.27	20.83	23.44	25.00
7.75	10.20	10.47	10.76	11.07	11.40	11.74	12.30	12.70	13.60	13.84	15.20	16.85	17.22	18.90	20.95	21.53	24.22	25.83
8.00	10.53	10.81	11.11	11.43	11.76	12.12	12.70	13.11	14.04	14.29	15.69	17.39	17.78	19.51	21.62	22.22	25.00	26.67
8.25	10.86	11.15	11.46	11.79	12.13	12.50	13.10	13.52	14.47	14.73	16.18	17.93	18.33	20.12	22.30	22.92	25.78	27.50
8.50	11.18	11.49	11.81	12.14	12.50	12.88	13.49	13.93	14.91	15.18	16.67	18.48	18.89	20.73	22.97	23.61	26.56	28.33
8.75	11.51	11.82	12.15	12.50	12.87	13.26	13.89	14.34	15.35	15.62	17.16	19.02	19.44	21.34	23.65	24.31	27.34	29.17
9.00	11.84	12.16	12.50	12.86	13.24	13.64	14.29	14.75	15.79	16.07	17.65	19.57	20.00	21.95	24.32	25.00	28.13	30.00
9.25	12.17	12.50	12.84	13.21	13.60	14.02	14.68	15.16	16.23	16.52	18.14	20.11	20.56	22.56	25.00	25.69	28.91	30.83
9.50	12.50	12.84	13.19	13.57	13.97	14.39	15.08	15.57	16.67	16.96	18.63	20.65	21.11	23.17	25.68	26.39	29.69	31.67
9.75	12.83	13.18	13.54	13.93	14.34	14.77	15.48	15.98	17.11	17.41	19.12	21.20	21.67	23.78	26.35	27.08	30.47	32.50
10.00	13.16	13.51	13.89	14.29	14.71	15.15	15.87	16.39	17.54	17.86	19.61	21.74	22.22	24.39	27.03	27.78	31.25	33.33
10.25	13.49	13.85	14.24	14.64	15.07	15.53	16.27	16.80	17.98	18.30	20.10	22.28	22.78	25.00	27.70	28.47	32.03	34.17
10.50	13.82	14.19	14.58	15.00	15.44	15.91	16.67	17.21	18.42	18.75	20.59	22.83	23.33	25.61	28.38	29.17	32.81	35.00
10.75	14.14	14.53	14.93	15.36	15.81	16.29	17.06	17.62	18.86	19.20	21.08	23.37	23.89	26.22	29.05	29.86	33.59	35.83
11.00	14.47	14.86	15.28	15.71	16.18	16.67	17.46	18.03	19.30	19.64	21.57	23.91	24.44	26.83	29.73	30.56	34.38	36.67
11.25	14.80	15.20	15.62	16.07	16.54	17.05	17.86	18.44	19.74	20.09	22.06	24.46	25.00	27.44	30.41	31.25	35.16	37.50
11.50	15.13	15.54	15.97	16.43	16.91	17.42	18.25	18.85	20.18	20.54	22.55	25.00	25.56	28.05	31.08	31.94	35.94	38.33
11.75	15.46	15.88	16.32	16.79	17.28	17.80	18.65	19.26	20.61	20.98	23.04	25.54	26.11	28.66	31.76	32.64	36.71	39.17
12.00	15.79	16.22	16.67	17.14	17.65	18.18	19.05	19.67	21.05	21.43	23.53	26.09	26.66	29.27	32.43	33.33	37.50	40.00

Source: "39 Tax Savings Ideas for Investors." Copyright, Merrill Lynch Pierce Fenner & Smith, Inc., September, 1980.

The tax tables have not been adjusted for our inflation-bloated incomes. The result is that tax tables established for an earlier generation are being applied to us today and our incomes don't allow us to live as these incomes would have when those tax tables were conceived. If your parents in their working prime made the money we do today, they would have been able to live twice or three times as well as we do. The tax tables may have been fair then but they are certainly unfair now because they haven't been adjusted for inflation.

Inflation is the reason every investor must search for means of lifting the heavy weight of income taxes from his shoulders. While Congress debates what is deductible and what is not, a simple 1 percent rise in the inflation rate means an additional 1 1/2 percent increase in your tax bill. Because tax brackets haven't been adjusted for inflation, if you are an average American, you work until the month of May each year just to pay your Social Security and income tax bill. Obviously then, it is important for your investments to at least keep pace with inflation.

Suppose you and your spouse earn $40,000 a year, have some taxable dividends from savings of another $2,000 to $3,000 a year. According to the chart, after you subtract some typical deductions you are in the 34 percent to 37 percent tax bracket. The $2,000 to $3,000 dividends are being clobbered by the IRS like this:

$3,000	dividends
$ 400	marital deduction
$2,600	taxable
37%	tax bracket
$ 962	tax
$1,638	left after tax

Most people can't believe the tax bracket they are in. And make-believe examples are never as powerful as the one that involves you. Take a minute now and check last year's tax return. Look at the chart and see what tax bracket you are in and figure just how big the tax bite is on your interest or dividend earnings. It is easy to do the calculation yourself. Here is how.

$10,000	investment	_____	your investment
7%	saving account	_____	interest rate paid
$ 700	before tax earnings	_____	before tax earnings
× 37%	tax bracket	_____	multiply by tax bracket from chart
$259	tax owed	_____	tax owed
$ 700		_____	before tax earnings
− 259		_____	less taxes
$ 441	after tax return	_____	after tax return

In this example $441 represents a 4.41 percent after tax return on investment. You need only *better* that rate with a tax-free investment to improve your investment return.

In fact, you need only *equal* that rate (4.41 percent) to be better off earning tax-free income. I tell people that because the effect of earning tax-free income is one of lowering your overall tax bracket. If the $10,000 invested in my example at 7 percent taxable was invested instead in something that didn't produce taxable income, the effect would be that your overall tax bracket would be lower.

	70%
	60%
_____	
DIVIDENDS	50%
_____	40%
INTEREST	30%
_____	
SALARY	20%
_____	_____
INCOME	TAX BRACKET

As your interest and dividend income rise, so does your tax bracket. The thermometer shows how you compound your tax problem by adding on top of your earned income (your salary), the other taxable income such as dividends, interest, and other money that your savings buys for you. Additional income pushes you into a higher and higher income tax bracket. By investing in tax-free securities, you remove some of the layers that force your income tax bracket higher. As you can see, by switching from investments that buy taxable income to those that buy tax-free income you will lower your income tax bracket. Imagine how much more quickly you will be able to build your savings program if you can do it without contributing such a large share to the IRS.

A High Return Is More Important Now than Ever

Of all the forecasts for rate of inflation in the 1980s, not one of the experts I've asked believes the rate will be zero. Assume you are able to get an 8 percent return after taxes. That sounds like a decent return. But see what happens to your purchasing power given these inflation rates.

	Growth of $1,000 compounded at 8%	*Purchasing power in 1980 dollars at these inflation rates*		
		5%	*10%*	*15%*
1981	$1,080	$1,028	$982	$940
1982	1,166	1,058	963	881
1983	1,260	1,089	946	829
1984	1,360	1,119	929	778
1985	1,469	1,152	912	730
1986	1,587	1,184	895	686
1987	1,714	1,219	879	644
1988	1,851	1,253	864	605
1989	1,999	1,289	848	568
1990	2,159	1,326	833	533

Up to this point my purpose has been to show you why you need to look to investments that are tax advantaged if you are in the 30 percent tax bracket or higher. There are a number of investments that qualify. Keep in mind that there is nothing sinful about buying money that is tax free or tax deferred. By reinvesting the money that would otherwise go to taxes, you can use it in your behalf as productive capital.

Ways to Buy Tax-Free Money

There are a number of ways to buy money that is lightly taxed by the IRS. These methods are all important to you. I will cover them in detail. However, there is only one *legal* way to buy money on which you will never owe a cent in federal income taxes and, in many instances, any state income tax. That is by investing in tax-free bonds and notes.

These tax-exempt securities are also called *municipal bonds and notes* because they represent borrowings by state and local governments and their agencies.

Investors are attracted to municipal bonds principally for the tax advantages, but also because, historically, they have proven to be safe places in which to invest. Even during the years of the Great Depression, less than two percent of municipal bonds ever went into default, and most of those were paid in full at a later date. The safety of municipal bonds is regarded as being second only to U.S. government bonds. Like all bonds, the price of municipals will fluctuate with changing interest rates.

Why Municipal Bonds Exist

Few communities have enough cash to build the schools or other major facilities they need. So they borrow the money. This is done by selling bonds to individual investors and to institutional investors such as banks and insurance companies. The special

57

feature about municipal bonds that makes them attractive to purchasers is that the interest the bonds pay, unlike the interest paid by U.S. government bonds or corporate bonds, is not taxed as income by the federal government. This is obviously advantageous to those who receive the interest payments. But it is also advantageous to the community that sold the bond. By being able to offer the purchaser the tax-free interest advantage, the community is able to borrow at a lower rate of interest. Therefore, the taxpayers of the community benefit from smaller local tax bills than if the interest rate paid by the community was as high as that paid by other borrowers, such as a corporation.

Types of Municipal Bonds

There are many types of municipal bonds, but they all fall into two main categories: *general obligation bonds* or *revenue bonds*. The difference is determined by the guarantee behind the bond. If the community borrowing the money pledges its full faith and credit to pay the interest when owed and redeem the bond when due, that bond is considered a *general obligation bond*. Taxes, in whatever amounts required, must be levied by that community to make the interest payments of the bond when they are due.

If the same community establishes a water authority to provide water and sewage service for its residents, the water authority as a separate agency of the community could borrow money to build its pumping facility and other necessary equipment. The water authority would issue and guarantee its own municipal bonds. It would be responsible for making interest payments to those who purchased its bonds and to repay the principal upon maturity. This is called a *revenue bond*, because the interest and principal payments will be made from the revenue earned by the water authority. The risk for your investment is that if not enough money is earned by the water authority, the bond holders will not receive the money owed to them. The community is *not* responsible for making up the difference since the bond is guaranteed only by the water authority.

If the bond were guaranteed by both the community and the water authority, it would be called a *double barrel bond.* So if the money owed was not earned by the water authority, the community would be required to make up the difference. Occasionally, a double barrel bond is backed by two separate revenue sources. Then, of course, the bond would have more than one guarantor.

Another type of revenue bond is one that is payable from a specific tax, such as a gasoline tax. There are also municipal bonds backed by corporations. These are called either *industrial revenue development bonds* or *pollution control revenue bonds.*

Pollution Control Revenue Bonds (PCR) In order to meet the clean air standards specified by the Federal Environmental Protection Agency, the utility company in your city has probably installed costly equipment in the plant. To make this expense less costly to your utility, the federal government has allowed the utility to borrow the money by using a form of municipal bonds. Thus, the pain of borrowing is considerably less for the utility. The bond might well be called the Leland, Michigan, Pollution Control Bond, for example. The only guarantor is the utility company. The town has simply lent its name to the bond. It is, in effect, a tax-free corporate bond.

Industrial Development Revenue Bonds (IDR) Another way a community can lend its name to a municipal bond, and yet have no financial responsibility to the bond buyer, would be through a bond called an industrial development revenue bond. This bond is also guaranteed by a corporation rather than the municipality. By law, its size cannot exceed 5 million dollars, which is considered a small amount in the bond market. Its purpose is to encourage corporations to open industrial facilities in a community. Coca-Cola Bottling, for example, could use the industrial revenue bond financing to raise money to build a bottling plant in Leland, if both the town and Coca-Cola agreed.

Leland might encourage this method because the new plant would mean additional jobs for the townspeople and additional tax revenue from the plant's sales. Coca-Cola might find such financing attractive because the municipal borrowing rate is generally the cheapest available to them.

How to Own Tax-Free Bonds

Municipal bonds are sold in five-bond units. When they are first issued, each bond is worth $1,000 and the five-bond unit is worth $5,000. This is the standard denomination in the municipal bond market and you should never buy anything other than a five-bond unit as it is not easy to sell a nonstandard unit.

Municipal bonds pay interest twice a year—on the anniversary of their issue date and six months from that date. Most bonds pay interest on the first day of the month. Those that don't, pay interest on the fifteenth day of the month. When you see a bond with this description: "7% Jun 90" it means that the bond pays 7 percent interest annually, on the first day of June and six months from that date, which would be the first day of December every year. It also tells you that the bond matures on the first day of June 1990.

Only when the number 15 is used after the month in the bond description, is the interest date other than the first day of the month. If no day is used, the first day of the month is assumed to be the interest payment date.

> Example: 7% Jun 15, 90
>
> Interest payment dates: June 15 and December 15
>
> Maturity date: June 15, 1990

Tax-free Bond Funds and Unit Trusts

Just as corporate bonds and U.S. government bonds can be bought in packages, you can buy tax-free bonds in funds and in unit trusts. There are those that are made up of long-term (twenty years and more), intermediate-term, and short-term bonds (six months and less). It is even possible to buy money market funds made up of tax-free securities. Bond funds and unit trusts are described in detail in Chapter 2.

COUPON OR REGISTERED BONDS

Most people who buy stocks and bonds will choose to leave them in their account at their brokerage firm. It is possible to have the certificates delivered to you. Some come with your name printed on their face, indicating that you are the owner. These securities are referred to as *registered*. In addition to having your name printed on them, the *issuer* (which is a corporation in the case of corporate bonds, or a state or municipality in the case of municipal bonds) has your name on its records. When an interest payment is due to you it is mailed directly to you by the issuer.

Bonds that don't have your name printed on them are called *coupon* or *bearer* bonds. As the issuer has no record of who owns these bonds, when an interest payment is due you must clip the appropriate coupon and take it to a bank for payment. Any bank will do. You simply need to hand the coupon to a bank teller. Some banks charge for this service and some others will insist on mailing the payment to you rather than promptly paying you. Expect the quickest service from a bank that knows you.

Each coupon is dated in six-month intervals and will show a dollar amount representing interest due on that date. The amount is equal to one-half a year's interest.

Bearer or coupon bonds are unique securities to many investors. So let me take a moment to give the answers to some of the questions I am most frequently asked about them.

1. Since bearer bonds are like dollar bills, if you lose either the coupon or the bond you are out of luck, because ownership is not registered with the issuer.

2. If you don't turn the coupon in for payment on the interest payment date, the interest (represented by the coupon) will not earn any additional interest for you. Mark your calendar and turn your coupons in on time.

3. A bond with a past due coupon attached is not worth any more than one with the coupon removed. The coupon represents earned interest only. The bond has a value independent of any interest that has accumulated to the date of sale. On that date all interest due will be paid to the seller, not to the purchaser. (See *Accrued interest* in the Glossary in Chapter 11.)

Municipal Bonds Are Usually Coupon Bonds Corporate bonds are usually registered in your name and municipal bonds are usually not.

If people are worried about the bother of clipping coupons, I advise them to leave their securities in their brokerage account. Then you won't have to worry about whether they are registered or bearer bonds. The brokerage firm will clip the coupons for you and the Securities Investors Protection Corporation protects a value of up to $500,000 per account against theft or loss.

Registering Municipal Bonds If you want a municipal bond delivered to you registered, you must give your broker specific instructions. He can register the bonds in different ways. Registered to *principal* only means that the certificate will bear the name of the owner, but the coupons (for interest payments) will be attached with no name on them. Registered to *principal* and *interest* will be a certificate without coupons. Interest checks will be mailed directly to you. There is a caveat, however. If you request registered bonds, this may slow up a later sale, or force a later sale at a lower price, because many firms impose substantial charges to "deregister" a bond to make it marketable.

Selling Coupon Bonds Reputable brokerage firms and banks insist on *proof of ownership* before they will sell a coupon bond for you or even hold it for you in your securities account.

Proof of ownership could be either the purchase *confirmation* or the carbonized slip of paper attached to the bond when it is delivered to you. That slip describes your bond, lists a certificate number, and includes your name and address. Also acceptable is a brokerage firm's end-of-the-month statement showing that the bond was at one time in your account.

Getting a Fair Price for Your Municipal Bond

Whenever you sell any municipal bond check with two or three brokerage firms for a price. You will be amazed by how much prices vary. This is because the municipal bond market is inexact. Unlike the highly efficient New York Stock Exchange, the municipal bond market is dealer to dealer, each one attempting to make a profit in the purchase from you and eventual resale. The bond you are selling may not have been sold by anyone else for several months as there are so many different bond issues. The dealer's perception of your bond's desirability may vary. Always get a price from a brokerage firm with offices near the municipality the bond represents. That firm should know the bond best and the demand is greatest in the bond's local area. Brokerage firms' policies and marketing capabilities differ and there can be errors made by the trader of any firm. Also, different commissions are charged by different firms and since prices are quoted "net," which means including commission, this can affect the selling price. By checking with several firms for the price you could realize a significantly larger amount of money from the sale.

Reasons People Buy Municipal Bonds

These are the reasons in capsule form:
1. *Safe investment* (if held to maturity and if viable)—The holder of a municipal bond has the issuer's promise to pay the principal and interest, as specified in the indenture

printed on the bond itself. In most instances, a state or municipality or agency pledges its entire earning resources to the payment of its obligations; in others, revenues from a specific project or utility secure the bonds. Either way, the issuer backs its bonds to the limit with its integrity.

2. *Excellent payment record*—In the darkest days of the depression of the 1930s, less than 2 percent of outstanding municipal bonds issued defaulted, and most of these were subsequently cleared up without loss of principal or interest.

3. *Tax exemption*—The major attraction of municipal bonds is their exemption from federal income tax. While income from corporate and other securities is subject to federal income taxes ranging up to 70 percent, the interest on municipal bonds enjoys complete exemption from these taxes.

4. *High collateral value*—In most instances it is possible to borrow up to 80 percent through 90 percent of the market value of your municipal bonds by using them as collateral, since most lenders, including banks and brokerage firms, recognize their quality and liquidity.

5. *Diversification*—Municipal bonds offer diversification in the broadest sense of the word. Geographically, literally thousands of communities, as well as virtually all the states, enter the market for funds each year. This allows the investor to select issues that suit his requirements for quality, and yield.

6. *Marketability*—Municipal bonds have always enjoyed good marketability. The evolution of communication in the municipal field similarly has reached a point where, through telephone and wire systems, brokers and dealers are virtually in constant touch with each other, producing a nationwide market for your bonds on an instant's notice.

7. *Wide selection of maturities*—Most municipal obligations are scheduled to mature over a period of years, enabling the borrowing communities to spread the tax burden, so

that subsequent as well as current users of the new facilities will share the construction cost. This feature is a boon to the investor who may wish to put his money to work for a specific period of time. The investor may obtain maturities that suit his estate building or educational plans, or for retirement purposes.

8. *Stability of ownership*—Since price stability is directly related to the stability of owners, it's important to note that holders of municipals comprise professional people, wealthy families, commercial banks, trusts and estates, insurance companies, and large corporations. All rely heavily on the soundness of municipals, as well as the tax-exemption feature. Speculators are not attracted to these securities because of this stable base.

9. *Double tax benefits*—In addition to their celebrated exemption from federal income taxes, municipal interest is usually exempt from state and local income taxes, providing the taxpayer is a resident of the state that issued the bonds. For example, Virginia does not tax interest earned by its residents from municipal bonds issued by Virginia municipalities. But you should check on this exemption before purchase.

10. *Tax exemption guaranteed*—The federal income tax exemption feature of municipal bonds is not a gimmick or tax loophole. Rather, it is based upon constitutional law.

11. *Insurance protection*—Municipal bonds are unique in that insurance is available that provides if the issuer fails to pay interest and principal when due, the holder can present such matured interest coupons and/or bonds to the insurer and obtain payment. The cost of coverage is about ½ of 1 percent in return. There are issues that are insured at the time of issuance. The coverage extends for the life of the bonds and has the same protection described above. This is paid for by the issuer or the underwriter. Your broker can provide information about insured municipal bonds and put you in touch with companies that offer municipal portfolio insurance.

12. *U.S. government-guaranteed municipal bonds*—The ultimate insurance program in the world of investments is the direct guarantee of the U.S. government, and this is available on some tax-free bonds that are issued by local *public housing authorities.* Bonds of this sort are excellent tax-free investments for those who feel comfortable investing only in U.S. government-backed securities.

The Lake Barcroft Story

You have just finished reading what you need to know about municipal bonds to be able to invest in them. However, there is a story behind each municipal bond certificate that you receive in exchange for your "investment." The following story illustrates the process of how a municipal bond comes into existence. Whether the bond issue is a large one involving hundreds of millions of dollars, or a relatively small one, the steps taken by a community to bring the bond into being are the same. This is how it's done:

Our hypothetical case began when tropical storm Agnes ripped through the eastern part of the United States in June 1972 leaving in its wake widespread destruction. Among the properties destroyed was a small earthen dam, the purpose of which was to contain the waters of a man-made lake called Barcroft. Built in the early 1900s as a water reservoir for the historic city of Alexandria, Virginia, the lake was sold to the residents of the surrounding area when it was no longer needed for that purpose. The dam, the lake and the recreational facilities surrounding the lake were maintained by the dues-paying residents of the houses around the lake. It quite obviously enhanced the property value of the area and was the focal point of community activities.

When the fierce winds of Agnes ruptured the dam, spilling out the lake water, all that remained was a 135-acre mud hole.

Quite naturally, the community wanted to restore the lake—but lakes and dams don't come cheap. The lowest estimated cost of repair was a bit over 2 million dollars. If each of the one thousand homeowners in the association were to divide the cost, a $2,000 assessment per home would have resulted. While that was a possible solution, getting one thousand homeowners to voluntarily assess themselves a large chunk of money is extremely difficult. As you would expect, the homeowners with "mudfront" property were a good deal more anxious to agree to the assessment than those several blocks away, but no one was anxious to pay the assessment.

Neither Fairfax County, the home of the Lake Barcroft Community, nor the Commonwealth of Virginia would pay for the lake's restoration because it was owned by a private community. Even the Federal Environmental Protection Agency refused to help the community out. The only remaining option was for the community to borrow the necessary funds and rebuild the dam itself. A bank was one possible source of funds, a municipal bond issue another. To satisfy Virginia law, the Lake Barcroft area was designated a watershed improvement district and was then given the authority by the state to issue the bond.

From the standpoint of the homeowners who would have to repay the loan, the lowest cost loan was the most desirable. Municipal bond loans are always cheaper than bank loans because the investors who buy municipal bonds are attracted by the tax-free interest those bonds pay. (Remember the previous discussion of the benefit of tax-free versus taxable interest to the investor; even though the interest rate is lower, it is more favorable to the high tax bracket investor.)

After qualifying to borrow as a municipality, Lake Barcroft hired an *investment banking firm* to assess the community's ability to make payments on a loan and then applied to a *rating service* to make a judgment about the relative quality of the borrowing. Standard and Poor's rating service gave the proposed bond a "BBB" rating, which is considered lower-medium grade. The rating determines the interest rate cost to the community. A better rating could have saved Lake Barcroft residents tens of thousands of dollars in interest payments a year, but the community was small and the rating awarded by Standard and Poor's was based on its many years of experience in judging similar communities throughout the country. Fairfax County agreed to collect the interest payment by adding a surcharge to the Lake Barcroft homeowners' property tax bill.

After all of these steps were taken, firm bids were sought from many construction companies, attorneys drew up the contract between the homeowners and the community, and a *prospectus* was offered that completely described the borrowing. A prospectus is written for all "revenue" municipal bond offerings and is available through brokerage firms.

A *legal opinion* is made after all the applicable state laws are reviewed to make certain that the issuer has the authority to issue such a bond, that the state has approved that particular bond, and that the contract between the bond owners and the bond issuers is proper. The legal opinion is found in the prospectus, and it assures the bond owner of a legitimate legal claim on the bond issuers.

The term *recognized attorney* is used because there are only some three hundred law firms in the country that have been judged by investment banking firms to be competent in this area. It is a highly specialized field and not just any attorney will do.

A *bid sheet* was prepared by the community's financial adviser so that the opportunity could be given to the entire investment community to bid on selling the bonds.

While the bid sheet is sent to nearly every investment banking firm, only those interested will return the bid form. Their primary considerations are (1) the profit they will make marketing the bond, and (2) ability to *easily* sell the bonds. Those firms with strong sales organizations in the Washington, D.C. area where the Lake Barcroft name would be recognized were the securities dealers most interested in the bond.

While investment banking firms were interested in high profit, Lake Barcroft was keenly interested in the lowest possible cost. This is why competitive bids were sought.

When they returned the bid form, interested investment banking firms also submitted a treasurer's check for an agreed amount. The check of the lowest bidding investment banker is kept as a binder. After the bid has been accepted, the bonds can be offered to the general public. Arriving at the bid is quickly done by the experienced bond dealers of the investment banking firms. They know the market for similar issues, as well as current interest rates, and place their bid accordingly. In a *competitive bid* deal, the investment banker must pay the issuer of the bond full value (par). Had Lake Barcroft *negotiated* with an investment banker for the sale of the bond rather than asked for bids, the community would have sold the bonds at a discount to the investment banker. His profit would have been the markup as well. All the *long-term* bonds are generally sold to the public at par (no markup). The shorter term bonds, or *serials* as they are called, are priced above par (this is where their profit is made), and are generally purchased by banks and insurance companies.

Remember, the community is interested in the lowest possible overall cost. That is, the lowest annual interest payment. Prospective bond buyers are interested in the highest possible return (rate of interest) on their money. The investment banker wants to make a profit after expenses—including sales commissions—have been paid. So, in submitting his bid on the bid form, the investment banker attempts to balance all of these considerations. The bidder with the lowest cost will be chosen by the community.

Investment bankers don't bid on an issue by themselves because they don't want to shoulder the entire risk and they generally need help selling the bonds, so they form a *selling syndicate*. Lake Barcroft, the issuing community in this case, deals only with the manager in the sale of its bonds.

The issuers must hire two other organizations for the life of the bond issue, a *registrar* and a *trustee*. These functions are usually performed by banks. If the issue is a small one, one bank may be both. The registrar pays the interest when due and maintains a record of the owners of the *registered bonds*. The trustee represents the bond owners, making certain that the contract is lived up to by the borrower and taking action if it is not. Both functions are paid for by the borrower. The fee to the registrar is usually twenty-five cents to seventy-five cents for each coupon redeemed, plus use of the money paid to it by the issuer until it is paid out to the bond holders. Sometimes this *float* can be quite meaningful, as the issuer is required to pay the registrar five days before the interest payments are due to the bond holders. Also, many individuals turn in the coupons to receive their interest payment after the coupon date.

When the bonds are first sold, they are usually labeled *when, as, and if* issued. This is a limbo period when investors have made a commitment to purchase the bonds, and the securities firm a commitment to sell them, but no money changes hands because during the period the final prospectus and the bonds are being printed. The bond itself is quite an interesting document. Besides the face value and maturity, the terms of the contract, size of the bond issue; name of the trustee; authorization under the state code; conditions; call provisions and legal provisions; and legal opinion are usually printed on the certificate. Each is hand signed by the head of the issuing authority. And after it is printed, the plates are destroyed. When this has all been done, the issuer turns the bonds over to the investment banker, who distributes them to the brokerage firms that sold them. Bonds in coupon form are mailed to the buyers immediately. Registered bonds are returned to the registrar to prepare.

Most of the buyers of the bonds were northern Virginians, including a good many Lake Barcroft residents. They were attracted to the investment by its tax-exempt return and because they were familiar with the Lake Barcroft area and believed it to be a sound risk. As it was a Virginia bond, the interest was state tax exempt to Virginia residents as well as federally tax exempt.

Remember that all municipal bonds are exempt from federal income tax. If they are issued by a municipality of the state in which you are a resident, then they are usually state tax exempt to you as well. States usually don't require that a state income tax be paid on their own municipal bonds. Bonds issued by Puerto Rico and the U.S. Virgin Islands are free from every state income tax.

The Lake Barcroft story explains how municipal bonds come into being. Each tax-exempt bond you buy or consider for purchase has a similar story. It is important to know that the bond is much more than a fancy certificate that pays interest twice a year.

5

Your Tax Bill Is Too High!

In 1913 Woodrow Wilson brought us the personal income tax. It was so simple and straightforward that everyone could understand it. The tax form was a single page. If your income was between $4,000 and $20,000, your tax was 1 percent of that amount. You paid an additional 1 percent tax on income between $20,000 and $50,000, and 2 percent on income between $50,000 and $75,000. You hit the maximum 6 percent bracket when your income exceeded $500,000.

Times have changed. Today that simple one-page tax form has been replaced with libraries of instruction, a language so cumbersome America has created a profession to decipher it, and an army of bureaucrats to enforce it.

No one argues with me when I say that their tax bills are too high. Yet few realize that there are things nearly everyone can do to reduce them.

Instead of buying money that increases your tax liability, it is possible for you to buy money that escapes the grasp of the IRS. It is also possible to postpone the tax bite on money you buy, or reduce it considerably. Keep in mind that a tax dollar you don't pay today is a dollar borrowed interest free. In addition to municipal bonds there are other sensible ways to invest to take advantage of the tax laws. This chapter focuses on the other tax-advantaged investment options that you should know. You might find one or two would fit nicely into your investment plan as well as favorably impact your tax bill.

Investing Through Your Children Can Be Better than Tax-free Bonds

Let's assume that your investment goal is to put aside money for your children's education. By saving in your name, *you* are responsible for paying the taxes on the interest your savings buy. *You* must pay the taxes based on *your* income tax bracket. However, if the money is in the children's names, *they* will pay the taxes based on *their* tax brackets. Unless your children are the Osmond Brothers or do a whale of a job selling lemonade, it is unlikely that their tax brackets are higher than yours.

So, by buying money in your children's rather than your name, you shift the income you receive from your investment from a higher tax bracket to a lower tax bracket.

This expands your investment options. For example, instead of buying a tax-free bond, which would make the most sense for you because you are a high tax bracket investor, you can buy a much higher yielding taxable bond or common stock or savings certificate. The tax your children pay on the income produced from that investment will be minimal.

You buy a $10,000 bond which yields 10 percent:

$10,000	bond
10%	return
$ 1,000	income
× 30%	tax bracket

$ 300	tax
$ 1,000	income
− 300	less tax
$ 700	after tax return

You buy for your child a $10,000 bond which yields 10 percent:

$10,000	bond
10%	return
$ 1,000	income

Assuming your child has no earned income, he or she may have as much as $1,000 unearned income without incurring any tax liability.

The procedure of giving the money to your children to invest is done under the *Uniform Gift to Minors Act* of your state of residence.

A good friend of mine, who is a CPA/tax attorney, tells of advising his father to use the Uniform Gift to Minors Act to shift income from his tax bracket to his daughter's bracket. She was in college at the time. Shortly after the transfer was made, the daughter dropped out of school, withdrew the college fund from the bank, bought a motorcycle, and set about discovering America, never to return to college. As my friend tells it, that was the last piece of financial planning advice his father has taken from him. The story points to the negative side of this tax savings strategy. That is, once the money has been transferred to the child's name, it is no longer the property of the parent. While the custodian has control of the investment when the child is a minor, the gift is the property of the child, and control passes from the custodian to the child as soon as he or she reaches the age of majority.

Uniform gift to minors accounts, or *custodian accounts* as they are called, are easy to establish. Your banker and broker should be familiar with the applicable laws. One simply needs to obtain a social security number for the child. An account can then be opened for the child with an adult as custodian at a bank or a securities brokerage firm.

There are certain restrictions that vary from state to state and the money given to the children is considered a gift. It is, therefore, subject to the gift tax laws. In the right circumstance, it is a nifty tool for the average investor with children or grandchildren. It can save you lots of money.

Lightly Taxed Income—Yes, Motorcycle—No!

What if you could put money into a tax-favored savings account or investment to fund the college education expenses of your children? The tax favor would be to have all of the income from that account taxed in the lower tax bracket of the children. After the children's education has been completed, whatever remains in the account would be returned to you.

This investment tool offers all of the advantages of the custodian account but, in addition, solves the custodian account's key disadvantage. That is, you never give up ownership of the principal. Such a program exists. It is called a *Clifford Trust,* a *reversionary trust,* or sometimes a *ten-year and a day trust,* the rules for which must be drawn up in a legal document by an attorney who is aware of the benefits and drawbacks of such an instrument. In essence, it says that the money in the account is to remain there until the purpose for the trust is satisfied, or until at least ten years and one day have passed. All of the income will be used for the purpose the trust has been established, such as the college education of the children in the family. The income will be taxed in the children's tax brackets as it is received by them. After all have been educated or decide that they don't want to be, the trust will be dissolved and the money will be returned. If the principal has appreciated because it was wisely invested during those years, that will be returned to the donor as well. Another useful purpose of the Clifford Trust is to provide support for an elderly dependent. As we are keenly aware, your money can go a good deal farther before it is taxed. For example, to spend one dollar at a nursing home, a person in the 50 percent tax bracket needs to earn two dollars. With the trust, the dollars received from the investments can go to the nursing home without being filtered through your high tax bracket.

Investors in oil and gas programs may be able to use the Clifford Trust to shelter the taxable portion of their cash distributions. It works like this. After the oil and gas program has been purchased and the deduction taken by the purchaser, the program is placed in the Clifford Trust. When income begins to come only the taxable portion of the income is paid out of the trust. The tax-free income remains in the trust to be distributed in lump sum after the trust is dissolved. Check with your accountant.

Once the trust has been set up by an attorney the account works like any savings or stock brokerage account. I have been asked time and again what such a trust looks like. Here is a sample trust document. State laws vary, as does the interpretation of the limits and use of such a trust. Should you decide to use one, check with your attorney.

DECLARATION OF TRUST

Made January 2, 1980, by

JOHN SMITH and MARY SMITH

1. *Trust Property.* We, JOHN SMITH and MARY SMITH, the Grantors, being residents of Smithville, Virginia, do hereby declare that we have received in trust, the following described property:

2. *Term.* This Trust shall continue for a term of ten (10) years and one (1) day from the date hereof, or until the death of both Beneficiaries, or upon the death of both Grantors, whichever occurs first.

3. *Trustees.* The Trust shall be administered by JOHN SMITH and MARY SMITH as co-Trustees, each having full authority to take any action as Trustee hereunder, either singly or jointly. No person purchasing the Trust Property or in any manner dealing with the Trust Property or with either Trustee shall be required to inquire into the authority of the Trustee to enter into any transaction, or to account for the application of any moneys paid to the Trustee in any account. Neither Trustee shall be required to post bond or be entitled to receive compensation for services performed.

4. *Beneficiaries.* The Beneficiaries shall be JOHN SMITH, JR. and JAN SMITH. If either Beneficiary shall pre-decease the other during the term of this Trust, his or her share shall accrue to the surviving Beneficiary. If the surviving Beneficiary shall also die during the term of this Trust, his or her interest shall accrue to his estate.

5. *Dispositive Provisions.* As Trustees under this Declaration of Trust, we shall hold, manage, invest, and reinvest the Trust Property, and shall collect the income therefrom, and after deducting all necessary expenses incident to the administration of this Trust, we shall dispose of the net income and principal as follows:

(a) *Income.* The net income shall be deposited to each or any of a savings, checking, or brokerage account in the name of JOHN SMITH and MARY SMITH as Trustees for the Beneficiaries herein, such funds to be used equally for the private school education or higher education of each of the Beneficiaries whose private school education or higher education has not been completed, and shall be accumulated for that purpose until needed; provided, however, that in no event shall the income be used to discharge either of the Grantors' obligation to support either of the Beneficiaries. Each Beneficiary shall be entitled to the net income from an undivided 50 percent of the Trust for the entire term of the Trust including income earned on accumulated income, subject to adjustment for distributions of corpus as provided in paragraph (6) below. No income shall be distributed from either Beneficiary's 50 percent interest for purposes other than private school or higher education of that Beneficiary until his or her education is complete; thereafter, each Beneficiary shall be paid his or her entire share of the income for the duration of this Trust. Upon termination of the Trust, all undistributed income shall be distributed to the Beneficiaries.

(b) *Principal.* The Principal, or corpus, of the Trust shall be subject to application at the election of either Trustee for the purpose of private school education or higher education of each of the Beneficiaries. The application of any part of the principal for the benefit of either Beneficiary shall reduce his or her share of income thereafter in proportion to the amount of corpus distributed. No application of principal shall be made to discharge either of the Grantors' obligation to support either of the Beneficiaries.

(c) *Reversion.* Upon termination of this Trust and distribution of income to the Beneficiaries, the remaining corpus shall be paid equally to the Grantors, or to the survivor, or to the estate of the survivor.

6. *Trustees' Powers.* In the administration of this Trust, we as Trustees, jointly and severally, shall have the following powers, all of which shall be exercised in a fiduciary capacity, primarily for the benefit of the Beneficiaries:

(a) To retain as an investment the Trust Property received hereunder.

(b) To sell and convey the Trust Property for such price and upon such terms as in our respective judgments may be deemed for the best interest of the Trust and the Beneficiaries, and to execute and deliver any contracts, assignments, or other instruments necessary in connection therewith.

(c) To invest and reinvest the Trust Property in securities or in investments of any kind, without being limited to Trust investments provided by law and without regard to diversification.

(d) To vote in person or by proxy the securities held by us as Trustees.

(e) To undertake any acts which in our respective judgments as Trustees are necessary or appropriate in the administration of this Trust.

79

7. *Limitation on Powers.* No powers enumerated herein or accorded to Trustees generally by law shall be construed to enable either of us, as Grantor, Trustee, or otherwise, or any person, to purchase, exchange, or otherwise deal with or dispose of the income or principal of this Trust for less than an adequate consideration in money or money's worth, or to enable either of us, as Grantor, Trustee, or otherwise, to borrow the income or principal of this Trust, directly or indirectly, without adequate interest or security, or to extend any loan that is not repayable by the end of the taxable year in which it is extended. No person, without the approval or the consent of either of the Trustees hereunder acting in his or her fiduciary capacity, shall exercise the power to vote or direct the voting of stock or other securities of this Trust, to control the investment of the Trust funds, or to reacquire the Trust corpus by substituting other property of equivalent value.

No portion of the income of the Trust shall be distributed to the Grantors, held or accumulated for future distribution to the Grantors, or applied to the payment of premiums on policies of insurance on the life of the Grantors.

8. *Principal and Income.*

(a) Extraordinary cash dividends, other than liquidating dividends, shall be income.

(b) All liquidating dividends shall be principal; but rights to subscribe to stock shall be treated as income.

(c) Dividends payable in stock of the corporation declaring the same shall be principal, except that any such dividends paid in lieu of periodic cash dividends shall be income.

(d) Dividends payable in stocks of a corporation other than the corporation declaring the same shall be income.

(e) All profits from sales, exchanges, or other dispositions of Trust Property shall be principal.

9. *Situs.* This Trust shall be construed and regulated according to the laws of the State of Virginia.

10. *Irrevocability.* This Trust is irrevocable and shall not be subject to alteration or amendment by the Grantors or any other person.

In witness whereof we have executed and acknowledged this Declaration of Trust.

Receive Your Share of Tax-free Dividends

Every taxpayer is allowed $200 of tax-free dividend income. A husband and wife filing jointly can excuse $400. Take advantage of this benefit by investing at least enough money in common or preferred stock to generate that amount of income. Because many stocks pay attractively high dividends, an investment in one can produce enough tax-free income to equal the amount received from investing twice as much money in municipal bonds.

Some Common Stocks Consistently Generate Tax-deferred Income

The dividends of many utility companies* are partially (in some cases fully) tax exempt. The amount of tax exemption and the list of eligible companies change every year, but this is a marvelous way to earn tax-favored income.

Many brokers find that when they recommend utility company stocks that pay partially tax-exempt dividends they are faced with explaining why. It is a difficult concept to explain, and because the explanation is botched up so often I want to take the time to make it clear to you.

To encourage investment in plants and equipment, the tax law allows companies to depreciate plants and equipment faster than they actually wear out. Utility companies* are allowed to carry two sets of accounting figures on their books. The first is a calculation for tax purposes of how much, because of depreciation, a plant and equipment are declining in value each year.

---

*A few other corporations such as real estate developers, energy concerns, and closed-end investment companies also qualify for this tax treatment.

81

Since they are allowed to write off the plant and equipment over a shorter period of time than they actually wear out, this figure is higher than the second calculation, which reflects their actual loss of value. The difference between these two figures affects the earnings of the company and is called a *construction allowance*.

Utility companies are also allowed to add to their earnings a figure that represents the additional earnings that would have been produced from dollars tied up in the construction of new plant and equipment. This is a phantom figure called *allowance for funds used during construction.*

These two numbers are added together and then added to the real earnings to determine the company's total earnings. The company then pays dividends out of the total corporate earnings, but since part of the dividends have been paid from the invested earnings (which is not taxable to the corporation), when it is paid to the shareholders it is also not taxable. Accountants consider it a *return of capital.* It is important for the shareholder to keep track of the total amount of capital that is returned to him and to reduce his original purchase price of the stock by that amount. At the time of sale the return of capital will be taxed as a long- or short-term capital gain depending on how long the stock was held before sale.

A problem with this tax-advantaged investment is the unpredictability of how much, if any, of a given utility's dividend will be tax exempt during the coming year. Just because a portion of the dividend is tax exempt this year is no guarantee that any of it will be exempt next year. Also, the tax status of the dividend usually isn't determined by the utility until one or two months after the year has ended. However, the list of possibilities can be narrowed because those companies involved in continuous expansion programs are likely candidates. A list of those companies can be obtained from many major brokerage firms. Ask as well about utilities that have long records of yearly dividend increases and those with the highest rates of compounded dividend growth. Obviously, those companies are good investment candidates.

Tax-deferred Annuities

Many people believe that savings certificates are the best choice for their investment program. An alternative that has many of the same features yet pays *tax-deferred* income is called a tax-deferred annuity.

Assume you have a few thousand dollars to invest. Assume further that: (1) you don't want to pay current income tax on the interest earned, (2) you don't need that interest now so you would like to leave it to compound, (3) you want your capital to be immediately available (liquid, in case of emergency), (4) if the need occurs, you would like to use it as collateral, and (5) you don't want to take the risk of getting back less than what you originally invested. A tax-deferred annuity might be your best investment choice.

These annuities are in reality loans *you* make to insurance companies. They earn interest that is credited to you but not taxable until it is withdrawn. Thus your investment compounds itself without being reduced by taxes. This means that your savings dollar will grow much faster than in most other programs. The stability of principal and liquidity of the investment are guaranteed by the life insurance company which, by law, must maintain cash reserves to cover withdrawals.

I told you that you can't make use of the interest earned on a single premium tax-deferred annuity without reporting the withdrawals as income, but it is possible to take occasional and random amounts until the entire original investment has been extracted, as this is considered return of principal. Only when the interest income is taken out is there a tax liability.

The major advantage of an investment in a tax-deferred annuity is your ability to compound interest before the IRS gets its share. The power of compound interest is almost unbelievable. When you let it work at a high rate of interest undiminished by taxes it can put you on the way to financial independence.

COMPOUNDING INTEREST

Consider this. Not only does your principal investment earn interest but the interest earns additional interest and the interest on interest earns interest. To put this in perspective, a $10,000 investment at 8 percent will, in thirty years, return the original $10,000 plus interest on the $10,000 which equals $800 multiplied by thirty years, or $25,000, plus interest on interest equal to $71,000. So the $10,000 would grow to $105,000.

What if you don't have $10,000 to invest now but could invest $1,000 a year for the next thirty years at 8 percent interest? That modest plan would net you $122,346.

Build a savings program you can live with using this compound interest chart.

COMPOUND INTEREST TABLE

One dollar per annum
paid in advance at the beginning of each year
will increase to the following amounts
at the rates of interest and in the terms designated

6%	Years	8%	10%	15%
1.060	1	1.080	1.100	1.150
2.184	2	2.246	2.310	2.473
3.375	3	3.506	3.641	3.993
4.637	4	4.867	5.105	5.742
5.975	5	6.336	6.716	7.754
7.394	6	7.923	8.487	10.067
8.897	7	9.637	10.436	12.727
10.491	8	11.488	12.579	15.786
12.181	9	13.487	14.937	19.304
13.972	10	15.645	17.531	23.349
15.870	11	17.977	20.384	28.002
17.882	12	20.495	23.523	33.352
20.015	13	23.215	26.975	39.505

COMPOUND INTEREST TABLE

One dollar per annum
paid in advance at the beginning of each year
will increase to the following amounts
at the rates of interest and in the terms designated

6%	Years	8%	10%	15%
22.276	14	26.452	30.772	46.580
24.673	15	29.324	34.950	54.717
27.213	16	32.750	39.545	64.075
29.906	17	36.450	44.599	74.836
32.760	18	40.446	50.159	87.212
35.786	19	44.762	56.275	101.444
38.993	20	49.423	63.002	117.810
42.392	21	54.457	70.403	136.632
45.996	22	59.893	78.543	158.276
49.816	23	65.765	87.497	183.168
53.865	24	72.106	97.347	211.793
58.156	25	78.954	108.182	244.712

For example if you could invest $2,000 a year at 10 percent for twenty years you would have 63.002 multiplied by $2,000 equals $126,004. What does it take to become a millionaire? If you are able to invest a little under $9,300 every year for twenty-five years at 10 percent interest you will be able to do it. Sound like a lot? It works out to less than $2.60 a day. How much do you spend for lunch?

The major drawback of the tax-deferred annuity is that the high guaranteed rate of interest is generally only for limited periods of time. After that time the guaranteed rate of most contracts drops to a very low rate.

Theoretically, the rate will be adjusted higher if interest rates generally are higher, so as to remain competitive. That doesn't necessarily happen. You could be forced to pay a withdrawal fee to get your funds out of the program. And the withdrawal fee is not tax deductible.

Other than withdrawing your funds you could continue to defer the tax liability on the interest you have earned by switching from one annuity to another anytime before you *annuitize* to receive a higher rate.

To annuitize means to select one of the insurance company's options for payment of the amount owed to you over a number of years. The amount the insurance company will pay you monthly depends on your life expectancy.

SELECTING AN ANNUITY OPTION PAYOUT

Traditional annuities are advertised as incomes you can't outlive. Once you annuitize, the insurance company guarantees to pay you a certain amount of income for as long as you live. Let's say that you are 65 years old and that the annuity you bought twenty years ago is now worth $100,000. The insurance company may estimate if you are a female that you will live 18.2 years.

AGES	MALE	FEMALE
65	15.0 years	18.2 years
66	14.4	17.5
67	13.8	16.9
68	13.2	16.2
69	12.6	15.6
70	12.1	15.0
71	11.6	14.4
72	11.0	13.8
73	10.5	13.2
74	10.1	12.6
75	9.6	12.1

Source: Internal Revenue Service Actuarial Tables

The company will therefore pay you an equal amount each month based on your life expectancy. If you outlive the projection, you would continue to receive payments nonetheless. If not, the payments would end early and the balance of the money in the annuity would belong to the insurance company.

If you have no one to whom you may leave your money, you might be better off selecting this payment option. But keep in mind that once you give up the principal amount it can never be recalled, regardless how bad inflation gets. To prevent the risk that you drop dead the day after choosing this annuity settlement option, you could select instead an option that allows for payments over your and your spouse's lifetimes, or a minimum of ten, fifteen, or twenty years. With this choice, should you both not live that number of years, your beneficiaries would continue to receive payments until that time is up.

YOU DON'T NEED TO ANNUITIZE

Remember, annuitizing is not the only way to take money out of your tax-deferred annuity. You can withdraw it all at one time. When you do, the interest income that has been accumulated will be taxable. If it is taxed all in one year, the effect could be devastating unless you are in a very modest tax bracket. It is also possible to remove the original investment without taxes and annuitize the remainder.

There are as many variables with this investment as there are insurance companies that offer them. Compare them very carefully. Check their fees, the withdrawal provisions, their guaranteed rates of interest, and the quality of the company behind the guarantee. These items vary so widely that your investigation should be thorough.

In my view, single premium tax-deferred annuities make the most sense to people who don't need the income from their investment now and who foresee some point in their lives when their tax bracket will be lower.

Classic Tax Shelters: Public Programs in Oil and Gas and Real Estate

These two kinds of programs have mushroomed in popularity because of their tax benefits and because many have proven to be excellent investments in their own right.

They are generally set up as limited partnerships. This is

because partnerships can pass directly to the individual partners all profits and losses. The general partner manages the business while the limited partners provide most of the capital—which is the extent of their involvement. There is no liability other than the dollars invested.

OIL AND GAS

Oil and gas partnerships allow the deduction of nearly all dollars invested, and, if oil or natural gas is found, substantial gains are possible. As the likelihood of finding a productive well is about one in fifteen drilling operations, the risk is high. But as oil and gas prices have skyrocketed, the rewards have also increased. Limited partnerships drill a number of wells, thus seeking to better their chances of being successful. If your program is a good one, it is possible to realize a substantial gain either from the income produced through the sale of oil and gas by the partnership, or by selling your interest.

The obvious risk involved in this shelter is that, if no oil or gas is found, the money invested is lost. A part of this money would have otherwise been paid in taxes. So part of the money you invested was Uncle Sam's, but the balance was yours. The higher your tax bracket, the fewer of your own dollars you put at risk and the more that would have gone to the IRS.

Any investment should be chosen on its own merits, with the tax dollar savings being a secondary benefit. Thus, investors should invest in oil and gas programs offered by reputable dealers with reputable firms. While the prospectus of each partnership is difficult to decipher for most people, a few questions to ask are:

1. How much of the investment is going into the ground and how much into the hands of the promoter?
2. Is the promoter committing himself to any of the costs?
3. What will the limited partner's share of the earnings be versus the general partner's if oil and gas are found? And
4. What is the experience of the general partner?

Another good general rule is to diversify among oil and gas programs, even if by the same general partner, to give yourself a better chance. The greater number of wells, the greater the opportunity for success. Most public oil and gas investment programs are available in $5,000 or $10,000 amounts. So if you have around $20,000 to invest in oil and gas programs, spread it around.

One interesting tax savings strategy that can be employed by investors in oil and gas programs concerns transfer of ownership. After drilling is completed by the general partner, the reserves are estimated and a liquidating value is established for each limited partner's interest. Typically, the first valuation a limited partner receives from his general partner is quite low. It is not unusual for a $10,000 investment to have an initial liquidating value of $2,000 to $3,000. As the investor, you have already taken the $10,000 deduction from your taxes and have, therefore, derived the biggest tax advantage.

Now you can give your interest to your child. As its value is less than the maximum gift allowed without tax consequence, there is no gift tax liability. Any appreciation from the first value will occur in your child's tax bracket.

If you are a successful oil and gas investor and the value of your partnership interest increases significantly—there is another option with favorable tax consequences that is open to you. Give it to your alma mater or charity! The full value of the appreciated asset is deductible, assuming you have held it for one year, even though it cost you far less.

REAL ESTATE

Real estate limited partnerships appear less formidable to understand than oil and gas because, unlike oil and gas wells, most people have some experience with real estate ownership. It doesn't mean that most are experts by any stretch of the imagination. There is no investment that is without risk. Some risks are less apparent than others.

A real estate partnership pools money it receives from limited partner investors to buy office buildings, shopping centers, or apartment houses. The rent paid by the tenants is passed along to the limited partners after the expenses have been paid. This surplus is referred to as a *positive cash flow.* Because the buildings in the partnership are *depreciated,* that income is generally *tax sheltered.*

Depreciation means that the building owners can say that the building is worth less each year because of wear and tear and take that amount as a deduction when computing their tax bill.

On one side of the balance sheet, there is a loss due to depreciation, and on the other, there is the income from the rent paid by the tenants. The limited partner receives his share of the rental income as additional taxable income but also his share of the loss caused by depreciation. The result is that the loss is generally equal to the income, so while he receives cash, he also benefits from the paper loss so that he won't have any additional tax liability.

The true advantage in a real estate program is that if the buildings can be sold for more than they were purchased, the limited partner stands to realize a capital gain. The difference between what the buildings are sold for and what they are worth after the total amount of depreciation has been subtracted from the original cost of the buildings is the capital gain or loss.

There are a host of risks in real estate as well as in oil and gas deals. There are competent general managers as well as those who don't belong in the business. There is the risk that the tenants will leave and the building will stand unrented. It is conceivable that, despite inflation, the building actually loses value or that the rents won't keep up with the expenses. It is also possible that no one will want to buy the building when the partnership wishes to sell it.

If there weren't any risks involved with tax-advantaged investments, there wouldn't be any legislated tax advantages. And, true of virtually all interests in limited partnership tax shelters, is that your share will be difficult to sell. They are highly illiquid! You should consider investing only those dollars you won't need to get your hands on quickly.

This brief description of oil and gas and real estate tax shelters is meant only to make you aware that such programs exist and that they are widely used. The subject is one best described in full-length books rather than in a small section of a single chapter. See the Bibliography for some recommended books about tax shelters. At least one is worth reading before you lay out $5,000 or more in any tax shelter program.

Make the IRS See Red

Every year you are allowed to deduct $3,000 of capital loss against ordinary income, after you have offset any capital gains. If you are in the 30 percent tax bracket this will save you $900 in taxes ($3,000 × 30% = $900). In the 50 percent tax bracket, it will save you $1,500 in taxes.

Many investors ignore this method of reducing their tax bills, and yet it can be done rather painlessly through a *tax swap.* A tax swap is an exchange of one investment for another similar investment below its original cost. It is usually done with bonds but can be done with common stocks. As an example, assume that you own a $10,000 face value bond which pays 8 percent interest and that its current market value is $7,000. The reason it is selling at $7,000 is probably because interest rates in general are higher than 8 percent, so all bonds yielding 8 percent of *similar quality* and *maturity* are selling at approximately the same price. By swapping your 8 percent bond for another similar bond, you have given up nothing. Your income will remain the same because 8 percent from one bond is the same as 8 percent from another. If interest rates in general move lower, one 8 percent bond will recover in price just as another. At maturity, both will be worth face value. Thus, the swap has not materially changed your investment. Instead of a bond from company X, you now own a bond from company Y. What you have done is establish a loss of $3,000 ($10,000 purchase price less $7,000 swap price), which can offset ordinary income and reduce your tax bill. By swapping it is meant that you have *sold* the bond you owned and *bought* a similar bond.

Some caveats of which you should be aware: the IRS will not allow the deduction if the bonds are identical. And long-term losses are worth only one-half of short-term losses so that in order to establish a $3,000 deduction against ordinary income, you will need to recognize a $6,000 long-term loss.

A key rule to remember is: take your losses early. Under existing legislation this means that you must take them in less than a year after purchase to qualify for the full benefit of the short-term loss.

The tax swap concept can be used to exchange one utility common stock for another, a steel company common stock for another, or whatever.

The other acceptable method of establishing the loss for tax purposes without giving up entirely on your investment is to sell the security and stay out of it for more than thirty days and then buy it back. If you believe that the market price of the security is unlikely to change much in that period of time, you risk little by being out of the security for thirty days. By getting back in it, you give yourself a chance to regain the lost money if the security should bounce back.

If you don't want to risk the chance that the security will move up in price without you owning it, you can *double up* for thirty-one days. By doubling up, it is meant that you buy an equal amount of the security in which you have the loss. After thirty-one days you sell the first lot you owned, leaving yourself with the same amount you started with. The loss equals the purchase price of the original investment less the sales price.

The thirty-day requirement has been set forth by the IRS to establish a risk. Short of that minimum time period any purchase or sale of substantially identical securities would be considered a *wash* transaction and, therefore, would not qualify you for any tax savings benefit.

If there are losses in your securities, you might as well take them to save yourself some tax dollars now. But keep in mind that if the security increases in value, you will be required to pay a capital gains tax on any appreciation when the security is sold at a gain at some later date.

6

The Stock Market

The kinds of financial tools I've described up to now are in many respects similar to savings accounts. They were not designed to be exciting investments. Most people, in fact, prefer their money to be working steadily in solid investments. Yet making money is exciting, and there is nothing quite like making a lot of it in a hurry.

Perhaps one of the most exciting places to make money is in the stock market. It can be fast paced, emotion packed, miraculously rewarding, or sickeningly depressing. It is mysterious not only to those who have never owned common stocks but unfortunately to many who do. That is why before reading about how to go about investing with common stocks it is important to understand what they are all about. Because to understand why common stocks exist is to appreciate the American economic system.

The basic difference between the American economic system and those systems that exist in other countries is the *source of capital*. In countries that are totally managed by government, the funds used to build factories and supply services come from the government. The amount of direct government participation in business varies from one country to another but in every

95

other nation the role of government in business is greater than in America. Our system is unique in that money for the development of business is raised from people and other private sources. Even more important, it comes voluntarily. It is not raised through taxes. In America, people labor to earn money and then have the opportunity to put that money to work for them to buy still more. Everyone has the same opportunity and it is possible for anyone to become financially successful. The system encourages initiative and enterprise. Stories of those who have designed new products, discovered better methods, promoted needed services, and have improved their condition in so doing can be counted in the hundreds of thousands. Our system is so unique that people from all over the world have flocked to America to participate in it. Nowhere but in America can a person be so handsomely rewarded for good ideas and hard work.

Ray Kroc, the founder of McDonald's, is a modern day testament to that fact. Columnist George F. Will wrote, "Ray Kroc is a small, energetic 75 year old who is as unpretentious as hamburger, as salty as french fries and as American as frozen apple pie. He is worth upwards of a half a billion dollars, which is not bad for a man who started his business when he was 52."

Ray Kroc didn't invent the hamburger nor did he build the first restaurant that sold them. What he did was build the empire that sold them best. Doing that took money, lots of it. The tale about how he raised that money illustrates how the American securities market works. It is a market of such instruments as *common stocks, private placement loans,* and *convertible subordinated debentures.* Knowing what each of these represents is somewhat useful to an investor, but definitions can be found in any dictionary. The McDonald's story is interesting because it puts securities in context. Instead of learning *what* they are, you should learn *why* they are.

There are important reasons they exist. They play a major role in your life whether you have ever invested in them or not. Because, like all businesses in America, McDonald's is not an island. If it stopped selling hamburgers, many thousands of people would be affected. Certainly those who are now employed by McDonald's would be, as well as those who sell McDonald's the buns, the ketchup, the meat, the uniforms, the glasses, and the plastic containers; and the people who work in factories producing those items, the farmers who raise the cattle and grow the lettuce, and the truck drivers who transport them. What about the companies that build the trucks and the gas station owners who supply their fuel? And don't forget the three to five cents on a dollar the state governments take in sales taxes. Employment in each of the businesses concerned is supported. People with jobs earn money, and because they do they are able to buy the items others produce and pay the income taxes levied by government. If you can picture this process as a wheel which goes around and around, you should have no trouble recognizing that the spokes of the wheel are securities. Without them the system we know today would not exist. This is why understanding the securities market is so important.

Back in the early 1950s only patrons of a quick service restaurant run by two brothers in San Bernardino, California, knew what it was like to chow down on McDonald's burgers. Then along came a salesman of multimixers—the milk shake mixing machine—to learn why one restaurant needed *eight* of his machines, since each machine was capable of simultaneously mixing five milk shakes. A typical restaurant was adequately served by one multimixer. As his company's top salesman, with such major clients as Dairy Queen, Tastee Freeze, and Howard Johnson's, Ray Kroc had visited a considerable number of restaurants, but the San Bernardino operation impressed him like no other. Patrons would line up for blocks day after day. The food was excellent—and it was fast.

Because he believed a McDonald's chain of restaurants could become another major market for his multimixer blenders, he tried to convince the McDonald brothers to open other restaurants exactly like it. When they declined, he bought the rights to franchise the restaurant from them. When he began selling the franchises, they went for $950 each. Today, if you can qualify for one be prepared to pay well over $200,000.

As a growing corporation, McDonald's made its money from the monthly fees it charged its franchise owners. Thus the larger the number of owners, the greater its profit potential. It was very much in the interest of the corporation to expand the number of McDonald's restaurants.

Working with one local bank at a time to build restaurants was not a terribly fast way to build a national restaurant chain. If Ray Kroc had not found other ways to raise money for expansion, you would probably not find a McDonald's restaurant today east of California.

So rather than obtaining one mortgage at a time from the banks, McDonald's sold packages of mortgages to insurance companies. These are called *private placements*.

Through the early history of the McDonald's Corporation all the restaurants were owned by the franchisees. Ray Kroc wanted to add some which would be company owned. This required a tremendous amount of money. Again, a group of insurance companies through private placement loans provided it. The loan was made at the going rate of interest with terms no more favorable than to any other client. But just to make the loan for the required 1½ million dollars, the insurance companies insisted on and received 22½ percent of the company's common stock. They wanted a piece of the ownership.

Ray Kroc said that the decision to give up that much of his company was one of the most difficult he had ever made. But to expand he needed the money and he couldn't get the money without giving up the stock.

At that time the common stock (representing the ownership of the company) was *closely held*. That means that it was owned by the founder of the company, Ray Kroc, and some other key people in the corporation. It was not owned by members of the general public. Obtaining this loan was the key to the growth of McDonald's, but the insurance companies who made it didn't fare poorly either. When they sold that stock a few years later, it brought them between 7 and 10 million dollars. Had they waited until now, their proceeds would have been over 500 million dollars.

Ownership is also referred to as *equity*. McDonald's transferred a large part of that equity from the founders to the public with the company's first *public offering*. Remember, the earlier financial arrangements with banks and insurance companies were private placements. Public offerings involve considerably more work on the part of the company because there are a host of government regulations to be adhered to designed to protect the public.

Ray Kroc had to make available all the pertinent financial records of the company, the background of the corporate officers, and other information important to would-be buyers of the corporation in an offering brochure called the *prospectus*.

Whenever any investor is offered a new stock or bond a copy of the offering prospectus is provided. It is a cumbersomely written document stuffed with legalistic language and dry detail. As a result, few people actually read it. The prospectus is prepared with the help of a company's *investment banker*. This is a securities firm that organizes the marketing of the common stock shares as well as determines what the fair market value of these shares on the offering will be.

A variety of considerations go into the marketing of a new common stock. Many are similar to the ones you would use to determine the sale price of your home. For example, what similar homes have sold for, what factors are that might make yours worth more or less, and what the minimum price is with which you would feel comfortable. The "what similar homes are selling for" issue in the securities field has to do with something called a *price earnings ratio*. Since not every fast-food restaurant chain stock sells for the same dollar amount at the same time, it was important to know the *earnings per share* of these publicly traded companies. This is a key common stock evaluating tool. It is determined by dividing the amount of money the company earned in a year by its total number of common stock shares.

Earnings, or *company profits,* are terms used interchangeably. Earnings of 220 million dollars for McDonald's, with 40 million shares of common stock, means earnings of $5.50 per share (220 million dollars divided by 40 million shares). Assuming the price of the stock was $50.00 a share, the price earnings ratio would equal $5.50 divided by $50.00, or an eleven to one price earnings ratio.

Unlike the selling of your home, a common stock can't be placed on the market for months waiting for the right buyer to happen by. The offering is usually made on one day through brokerage firms throughout the country, and then it begins trading in the *after market*. The quickest way to determine whether the price set in the offering was correct is to watch the way the stock trades after all the new shares have been sold. It is then that the shares are traded among those who bought them initially and others who want to own them. The price rises and falls based on demand and a variety of other factors, some rational and others emotional.

The initial McDonald's offering was very successful. The price of the stock rose from $22.50 a share on the offering to $30.00 by the end of the day and $50.00 by the end of the first month of public trading. These prices were substantially higher than the then-current earnings of the company justified. But the common stock buyers were buying in anticipation of future earnings and future growth. As it happened, their judgment was right. When common stocks sell out of line with a normally prudent price earnings ratio they are called *glamour stocks*. Some other well-known glamour stocks are Prime Computer, IBM, and Genetec.

Without the public offering, Ray Kroc would not have been able to raise enough money to be able to sustain the rate of growth he felt was necessary for McDonald's. A slower growth rate would have allowed competitors the advantage of catching McDonald's, or at least give those competitors the idea that McDonald's would be slow in serving the fast-food market that McDonald's proved existed.

The current price of McDonald's stock, as well as all publicly traded stock, is determined in the open market. Its price, like the price of your house, represents only what people are willing to pay for it. As groceries are sold in grocery stores, common stocks are sold in a market. While there are a number of different markets just as there are grocery stores, McDonald's stock was first sold in the *over-the-counter market*. This is not a place but a method of buying and selling the common stocks of most small or new companies. Because they are traded in this manner rather than on one of the exchanges, over-the-counter securities are referred to as *unlisted securities*. Conversely, those traded on a stock exchange are referred to as *listed securities*.

The over-the-counter market is a brokerage firm-to-brokerage firm method of handling the purchase and sale of unlisted common stocks. Certain brokerage firms will have enough interest in a particular company to *make a market* in that company's common stock. By make a market, it is meant that the brokerage firm under normal circumstances will use its own money to buy the stock of that company and have it available for sale should a buyer appear. Not every brokerage firm will make a market in every over-the-counter stock. For some stocks, only one or two firms will show that interest.

As it was traded over-the-counter, those people who sold shares of McDonald's stock purchased on the offering did not sell it to another individual but to a brokerage firm that made a market in the stock. That firm then sold it to another investor.

Usually common stock is traded this way because it has limited appeal. As interest in McDonald's grew, the common stock graduated to a stock exchange. Today it is traded on the largest securties market, the *New York Stock Exchange*.

It is at this marketplace that orders to buy and sell securities come from around the world. Unlike the over-the-counter market, which buys from one person and sells to another, the NYSE and the other exchanges don't buy and then sell securities. The NYSE is simply the place where the exchange of securities between buyer and seller occurs. It is more like a farmers' market than a grocery store. Orders to buy are matched with orders to sell. The NYSE reports each trade as it occurs, and in this way, the market price for each security is made public continuously.

Stockbrokers, the people through whom most buying and

selling of stocks is done, have video display computers which show each trade as it takes place on the NYSE and all the other markets on which stock is traded, as well as the over-the-counter market. By visiting a brokerage office, anyone can watch the trades as they occur.

As an owner of McDonald's Corporation common stock, you have a right to vote for the Board of Directors of the corporation. Obviously, those owners with the most shares will have the greater voice in the election. Also as an owner, you will receive an *annual report* which describes the past year's performance, the corporation's plans and programs. You may attend the annual meeting at which the Board of Directors election takes place, and you are entitled to receive any *dividends* which the Board decides to pay. A dividend is a share of the profits. Not all of the profits can be distributed, as the company must use some of that money to grow. Not all companies make a habit of paying dividends. If which do and which don't is important, you should check the dividend payment history of the company before investing in its common stock. As quarterly reports are made about the earnings of the corporation, so are quarterly dividend decisions made. Thus, if you own stock which pays cash dividends you will receive a check once every three months from the company. Many companies offer *stock reinvestment plans,* which allow you to buy additional shares of stock with the dividend money. Most times this is without a brokerage fee. Sometimes it is at a small discount to the market value of the stock. Some companies pay additional stock rather than cash. These are called *stock dividends.* Sometimes a company will decide to pay a very large stock dividend. This is also referred to as a *stock split*—for example, if a 100 percent stock dividend were declared—for every share of stock you own you will receive another share. In "the market" the effect of a two-for-one stock split is for the shares to be worth half of what they were before the split. Instead of owning one share worth $50, after the split you would own two shares worth $25 each. Companies have stock splits to make their stock more attractive. Stocks selling at $25 a share generally are more appealing to buyers than those selling at $50.

Because of stock dividends resulting from an exceptional record of growth, one share of McDonald's common stock purchased at $22.50 in 1965 would today be worth over $110,000. Not every company has enjoyed the same record, just as not every runner will win the Boston Marathon. Yet varying measures of success are possible, and the investors who buy shares of such companies can profit or lose as part owners of those companies.

Today, finding an American who hasn't sunk his teeth into a McDonald's hamburger could turn out to be as challenging as finding one who hasn't become bleary-eyed watching television. New generations of Americans grow up believing that the Big Mac is as much an American institution as apple pie. But without the securities markets this could not have been. The taste of the McDonald brothers' fantastic french fries and quick service hamburgers might belong only to those who happened by their busy restaurant in San Bernardino.

7

How to Buy Money with Common Stocks

I have described how to buy money with the lowest possible risk while pointing out that every investment involves some measure of risk. In the previous chapter I explained how common stocks and the stock market serve our economy. In this chapter I will focus on how those investments can serve you.

Is there risk investing in the market? Certainly there is risk, but the potential benefits may compensate for that risk. In periods of high inflation you must protect the buying power of your savings account. To do that you need some investments that have the potential to grow. Common stocks have that potential. And that is why you should know how they work and how to use them as part of your investment program.

As the market has been significantly undervalued for so many years, your chances of being successful now are higher than they have been in years. The decade of the 1980s may well be the market's most glowing yet. But those who approach it with lessons of the last two decades of market debacle planted firmly in mind may be the best equipped to reap the greatest success.

Presidential news conferences are always scheduled after 4:00 P.M. Eastern Standard Time. The stock market closes at

4:00 P.M. and what the President has to say can make the market react dramatically. Unfortunately, the President isn't the only one who possesses the ability to affect the market. *Forbes* magazine likens the stock market to a computer. "Its input is the knowledge, the calculation, the hopes, the fears, the dreams and the avarice of millions of investors." Its output is gyrating prices on a whole universe of common stocks. It is the most sensitive indicator to both good and bad news that exists. And like a weather-vane, its direction is nearly impossible to predict.

The stock market should be used by those who have in their character the ability to make decisions rationally when the world about them seems quite irrational. Because the stock market will test you like no place else, it is not a place to buy money for the faint hearted. As a common stock buyer, like a holiday gambler in Las Vegas, you should understand that you are not the most astute player at the table. You should also appreciate that logic does not often rule. Successful investors are professional decision makers rather than wafflers. They are aware that they are going to make mistakes and their professionalism doesn't allow them to react emotionally to those mistakes.

It is certainly true that many more people buy common stocks than those who fit the description. It is estimated that roughly 30 million Americans own common stocks. The stock market's reputation for being knotty doesn't stem from the notion that buying common stock is a difficult task. On the contrary, it is quite easy. The challenge is to *buy money in the process.*

How to Pick the Stocks to Own

What I tell my clients is to forget the idea that you have to love or even respect the company whose stock you buy. You aren't buying the company, you are buying common stock that happens to bear the company's name. You will never be able to own enough shares of the company for your involvement with that company to ever mean anything. To test the validity of this assertion, call your company, identify yourself as a shareholder, and offer some thoughtful suggestions about the company's operations. They will think you are crazy. Does General Motors give shareholders a discount on their Chevrolet purchase? Or does McDonald's give its owners a break on a Big Mac? Does any public company treat its shareholder customers any better than customers who don't own a part of the company? The disappointing answer in an overwhelming number of cases, is NO! Most companies have long since forgotten that they raise money by selling part ownership (common stock). They regard their public ownership as a burden. As an individual, you won't ever be able to own enough stock to affect any management decisions. And so by coming to grips with this reality, you can make yourself a better investor.

Accept also that you will rarely be the first to recognize a bargain in the market. IBMs, Xeroxes, and McDonald'ses don't come into being often. The trick is not to be the last to recognize value. A wise corporate management strategy is to let some other company be the pioneer. That is because pioneers make mistakes, spend several times as much money making the idea work as the second or third company that uses the same idea, and burn up lots of energy searching for a very small number of successful ideas.

This concept applied to the business of stock selection is translated: don't buy undervalued stocks before anyone else begins to buy them. Don't be a trend setter. Even if you are right and for some reason all the professional investors have missed them, you may sit on the stock quite a long while before the investment world recognizes its mistake.

Buy when the movement of money into the stock or industry group has already begun. Confirmation that the upward trend is about over is when some brokerage firm creates a mutual fund made up of those stocks.

READ *FORBES* MAGAZINE

There is absolutely no magazine better written for the investor than *Forbes*. From its pages dozens of good stock ideas leap out at you in every issue. Its computers spin out lists of stocks that fit nearly every investment criteria. No investor should go without the magazine.

As a common stock buyer, you must be open to a constant flow of ideas and make judgments about the merit of those ideas. From no other source will so many ideas flow so regularly.

READ THE BUSINESS SECTION OF A MAJOR PAPER

You must begin your morning with a copy of the *Wall Street Journal* or the *New York Times* business section, if you live in the New York area; this is a must. In Chicago it is the *Tribune* and in Los Angeles, the *Los Angeles Times*. Wherever you live you need the tools to work with your investments. The local paper's business section is essential. And, don't forget that stock market ideas come from the other sections of the paper as well.

CONSIDER *BARRONS*

Most Wall Street professionals spend part of their Sunday reading *Barrons*. It is a powerful financial weekly which is highly regarded by all those who work with securities for a living. If you want to hear about investments from your stock-broker's stockbroker, *Barrons* is the financial newspaper you will need to add to your reading list. Keep in mind that it is not written for those with casual knowledge about securities. It is filled with jargon and assumes a working knowledge of the lingo. To get the most from this publication, arm yourself with the Glossary of this book (see Chapter 11) for starters.

WATCH "WALL STREET WEEK"

This Public Television program featuring Louis Rukeyser and guests is the best half hour on television if you happen to like investing. Blending good-natured haughtiness and wit Rukeyser orchestrates this information-packed weekly showcase. By tuning in you will learn all you need to know about what happened to the stock market since last week's program. His panel of securities professionals (who are very likable people), answer written questions from viewers. During the last half of the program a discussion is held with a different guest each week. Topics focus on some aspect of investing in which there is current interest. If you haven't yet watched this program you have much to look forward to. Most investors love it!

OTHER INFORMATION SOURCES

Both Value Line and Standard and Poor's Corporation provide fact sheets on individual companies. Both are available in good libraries and most brokerage offices. Some advisory services are excellent. In addition to a brokerage company's research, which you can get at no expense, some of the advisory services to which you can subscribe are well worth the fee. In most cases, for an investor, fees for financial publications are deductible.

Whisper Stocks

Most legitimate stock buying ideas come to you in printed form from newspapers, magazines, and brokerage houses. The ones that come to you in a whisper, and hint at the possibility of merger, are the most dangerous of all. People listen because quick and sizeable fortunes are made through mergers and takeovers. But for every rumor that becomes fact, twenty produce sorry losers.

If you are to gamble in whisper stocks, at least follow these rules:

1. Stick with situations that don't depend on governmental sanction. Uncle Sam is not a quick decision maker.
2. Stay away from hostile deals—those that are opposed by the company being acquired. Even if the deal makes sense, it may be rejected.
3. Buy the stock only when you like it as an investment. If it sells substantially under its *book value*, an acquiring company may recognize it as being a bargain as well.

Remember, one bomb can wipe you out! A hot tip is usually worth every penny you paid for it.

Use Both Technical
and Fundamental Analysis

The purists will revolt at this statement claiming that these distinct methods of evaluating common stocks won't mix. The realists who have suffered through the market of the last two decades and watched every method of stock valuation be proven fallible, say otherwise.

From a fundamental standpoint, it makes sense to look for stocks with low price earnings ratio (p.e.'s). I suggest a price earnings ratio of 7 or less. The closer the price of a share of stock to its earnings the less downside risk there should be. If the stock is priced at $20 and the earnings are $5 a share, the price earnings ratio is 4. ($20 divided by $5). If the earnings go up to $7 a share and the stock maintains the same price earnings ratio, the stock will sell at $28 ($7 multiplied by 4 p.e.). If the price earnings ratio goes up to 7X (according to Benjamin Graham— *Securities Analysis*—that is an acceptable price earnings ratio), the stock would sell at $49 ($7 earnings multiplied by 7 p.e.). The fundamental benefits of low price earnings ratio and steady or rising earnings should produce a higher per share stock price.

If you own a stock with a very high price earnings ratio, you subject yourself to greater risk. Don't bet on future earnings by buying stocks which are selling at low p.e.'s "based on estimates" about future earnings. Buy stocks based on their current earnings. So much for fundamental analysis for the lay person investor. As for technical analysis, the market has spun in cycles and even the best stock will be affected by a down-trending market. Like Mosby's Rangers, you should be prepared to make your strike and disappear into the night.

Many fundamentalists will argue that you should buy a good stock and cling to it forever. The reasons this doesn't make sense are many. Consider the Dow Jones Industrial Average stocks for a few of those reasons. Assume that you bought these stocks in 1961 and held them over the past twenty-year period.

Surely there were opportunities to trade out of these stocks

PRICE FLUCTUATION

Stock	High	Low
Allied Chemical	62⅜	16⅛
Aluminum Co of America	72	24
American Brands	55¾	25⅛
American Can	64	22½
American Tel & Tel	75	39⅝
Eastman Kodak	151¾	20¼
Exxon	87⅞	19
General Electric	75⅞	27⅛
Westinghouse	54⅞	8
IBM	91¼	14½
Procter and Gamble	120	20½
Union Carbide	76¾	29¼
U.S. Steel	68⅞	16¾
Merck	101½	10

at profits, buy them back, and ride them awhile again. There simply is no sense in riding the roller coaster both ways. You should try to get out somewhere close to the top and climb on near the bottom. Take advantage of the cyclical nature of the market!

Neither the market nor an individual stock will move up or down without a correction. After the price has moved up for an extended period of time, be very careful about jumping on what may appear to be a bandwagon. Sell if you have a nice profit. Buy only after the stock has fallen off again.

Remember the lion hunt. Natives in a circle beat their drums to frighten the lion, causing him to run away from the noise into the muzzle of the hunter's rifle. Don't let the noise frighten you into a more dangerous position.

Find a Brilliant Broker

When you go into a court accused of murder you better have chosen a crackerjack lawyer. When you are diagnosed as being seriously ill, you will have a better chance of surviving if attended to by the best physician under the sun. When you invest your personal nest egg, you should hire the best stockbroker ever to lay his hand on a commission.

Being referred to a stockbroker is probably your best bet. A referral should come from people you respect, who you believe are successful investors. You can also ask your attorney or accountant. Then talk with your potential broker and try to judge his ability and experience. No stockbroker will be right all of the time. A good one has lost plenty of money as well as made plenty and learned from each experience. The story about experience is that some people have twenty years experience but it took them thirty-five years to get it. Others have twenty years experience but it has been the same one year's experience twenty times over.

The best brokers possess a "feel" for the market. This judgment or intuition or sense of the market is not infallible but can be extremely valuable to you.

You should seek one who is a good stock picker and market timer. It is especially useful to have one who speaks his own mind rather than echoing that of his firm, and will disagree with you when he believes your idea is a bad one.

If you don't use a stockbroker in this way, don't pay the exorbitant rates they all will charge you. If you generate your own ideas, make your own decisions, and can time your market moves without help, use a discount broker. You will save substantial commission dollars.

How Much Is Your Broker Worth?

A broker who is able to make 15 percent to 20 percent plus in your money annually for you after all fees have been subtracted is worth whatever you are paying him. Don't quibble about his fees because he is probably a financial genius and you are lucky to have found him and that he is willing to work with you. If consistent 15 percent to 20 percent-plus performance has not been your broker's track record and you are concerned about how much you are paying him, these ideas will be useful to you.

A stockbroker is paid like a physician or attorney—for his time. Time is worth different amounts to different people. Those whose incomes are high have generally placed a higher price tag on their time. Those with lower incomes may value their time less.

You should pay a broker for the time you use even though the system charges you by means of a "commission." How much you owe your broker should be computed this way. An average stockbroker will generate roughly $100,000 a year in commission business for his firm. Depending on the firm, between 30 percent and 45 percent of that amount will be paid to the stockbroker, but as a customer that is not your problem. The money you pay represents some part of the "total" commission and you, therefore, must use that amount to calculate what you owe for your stockbroker's time.

The market is open from 10:00 A.M. EST to 4:00 P.M., six hours a day, thirty hours a week. While it is usual that a stockbroker will work many more hours than these, most transactions take place during market hours. Since a broker is not paid for vacation or sick time, for the purpose of this calculation all fifty-two weeks will be considered. 52 weeks multiplied by 30 hours equals 1,560 hours divided into $100,000 equals $64.10 an hour, $32.05 a half hour, $16.02 fifteen minutes, $1.07 a minute.

If you are working with an average stockbroker, this is what you should be paying for his time through the commissions you generate with your brokerage transactions. If you are paying less than this amount, you are underpaying your stockbroker. If you are paying more than this, you are overpaying him.

Of course, there is value to the research and other written material he mails to you. There is also value to the safeguarding of your securities, to collecting and mailing your dividends and interest payments, as well as his handling money market and other transactions which involve no commission charges.

You could assign a plus or minus factor of 25 percent to the amount charged per hour if your broker is servicing your account especially well or poorly.

There should also be some consideration given to the amount of money your broker made for you, even though it wasn't as high as a 15 percent to 20 percent return on your investment. You should also consider the amount of tax dollars he saved you. These should be measured versus what you could have earned by simply leaving your money in the bank, less taxes. Add or subtract another arbitrary 10 percent to his hourly rate for every percentage point by which you beat the bank.

As an example, if your account has gained 10 percent versus the bank's guaranteed 7 percent, your broker's hourly rate would jump from $64.10 to $64.10 multiplied by 30 percent equaling $19.23 plus $64.10, or $83.33. And if you were especially well taken care of, add $64.10 multiplied by 25 percent, or $16.02, to the $83.33 figure. Your broker's hourly rate after these considerations is $99.35. You now have a basis of determining whether you are overpaying or underpaying your stockbroker.

While $100,000 annual commission earnings has been used in this calculation, some stockbrokers earn gross commissions of 1 million dollars per year, and it is not unusual to find stockbrokers whose gross commission earnings are between $200,000 and $500,000 per year. If you are working with one of these people, the amount of time he will be able to give you will obviously be much less for the same number of commission dollars. Is he worth it? From his perspective he is. So it is important as a client to determine at the beginning what price league you are in.

Pay Attention to Your Portfolio

Once you are in the market you have got to "stay alive." Like standing in the batter's box, the pitches keep coming. You've got to react to them all. Keep on top of your stocks and the market direction. Every day you decide to hold is as much a decision-making day as the day you decided to buy. Good news affecting the company may be an opportunity to sell. You may have heard the rule "sell on good news!" The thought is that since the good news is out, there is no more reason for the stock to go higher. Bad news may be a reason to buy more. The price may be pushed low enough to be especially attractive. The point is that news is certainly a reason to evaluate your holdings.

Sell!

Some people operate on Father Flanagan's theory that there is no such thing as a bad investment. That is not true. Your portfolio doesn't need to be a home for disadvantaged securities. As an investor you will find no end to the advice you will be given to "buy" various common stocks. Virtually every epistle from your brokerage firm, every investment magazine, and every call you receive from your stockbroker will concern itself with stocks you should be buying now. Stock buying is a public act. You will probably share your good judgment to buy various stocks with your office compatriots and at parties with friends. "I just bought five hundred shares of McDonald's," makes good cocktail conversation. It confirms your investment worldliness and your ability to recognize value. A "buy" is a positive act.

Stock selling, on the other hand, is a lonely experience. No glossy report will come from your brokerage firm, no list of stocks to be sold will appear in investment magazines, and don't hold your breath for your broker to call. But you have to sell to take profits and cut losses and to avoid the roller coaster ride down.

8

Some Basic Rules
for Buying Stock

Does it make sense to be in the stock market? You bet your antiques it does! Can money be made? It's not easy but it can be exciting and you don't have to wait around long to test whether or not your ideas have merit. The marketplace spits out its judgments quickly.

Successful stock market investors are a breed apart. They are "players" in a world of "spectators." Successful investors don't "wing" it. They play by a set of rules. This chapter explains some of those rules, which can be as effective to your investment program as it is to the pros. But keep in mind that the most difficult thing about investing rules is not understanding them but following them. Emotion can get in the way of common sense. And also keep in mind that there are no certainties in the market. One of the funny things about the stock market is that every time one person buys, another sells, and both think they have made the proper decision.

A good set of rules will help you be on the right side of a majority of your stock brokerage transactions, but of course there is no guarantee.

Invest So That You Can Sleep At Night

The first investment rule may be the most important of all. Every person who is about to buy money some place other than in a savings institution should spend time considering this rule: Know thyself! What sort of a risk taker are you? Investment return, after all, is a trade-off for risk. The higher the potential return, the greater the risk.

The mistake made by most investors is that when they consider investing, they focus attention on how much *reward* they need rather than how much *risk* they can comfortably tolerate. Once you understand how much risk you can sleep with, you are ready to buy money.

Pick investments that suit your character. Some investments don't have the potential of producing results quickly. Others won't pay any income while waiting for appreciation. Some others will pay a nice income but have no chance of growing. Some common stocks will bounce up and down like yo-yos, or be in the news constantly. Some of the news may take a cement stomach to tolerate. Make certain that your temperament matches the sort of investment you choose. And then set realistic objectives. As long as you are outperforming other alternatives, be pleased.

The best investment is "sleep through the night." If you choose an investment that causes you to lie awake worrying, then you have made a bad investment. Get rid of it and find some with which you can be comfortable.

If at First You Don't Succeed, Try to Hide Your Astonishment

The classic, yet most ignored rule of stock market investing is "take your losses early and let your profits run." No one buys a stock thinking it will go down. So the thinking results that, if it were a right decision to buy the stock at $15 a share, it must also be a good decision to hold it after it drops to $10. Since this is the way the average stock market investor thinks, you might be better off if you adopted this attitude: *Most of the stocks I pick are going to be losers.* However, a few will work out well enough to pay for my mistakes plus make this whole exercise worthwhile. To stay in the game, I've got to spot my losers quickly, get rid of them, and move the money into other situations.

By doing this, you will be more successful than the person who clings desperately to his original stock purchase—because his stock may drop to $5 after falling from $15 to $10. And when this happens, he feels trapped. How can he sell a stock at $5 a share that cost him $15? How can he justify a 66 percent loss? So he doesn't sell! His money will remain locked in that stock while he waits for it to move high enough so that he can "get even." He will be sitting on his hands as other investment opportunities come and go. Eventually, he will give up hope that his "dog," as he now calls it, will ever go up. He loses interest and joins the legion of investors who have had similar experiences. He vows never to go back into the market.

Meanwhile, you are still a "player." The stock that you bought at $15 was sold when it fell to $12. Twelve dollars was not a number arrived at through any elaborate mathematical model, but was simply a price beyond which you wouldn't feel comfortable watching the stock drop.

You bought the stock originally because you thought it would go up. You paid $15 because you didn't think it would be possible to buy it at $14⅞. Since it turned out that you were right about being wrong about most of your stock picks, and this was one, you sold it. And since you were not astonished to be wrong, your ego was protected.

Importantly, you took the loss while it was still tolerable. By allowing the three-point drop, you recognized that the stock price might fluctuate within a narrow band after you made your purchase. Few of us, after all, will be able to buy at the absolute bottom or sell at the very top. That is because bells don't toll, lights don't flash, and there are no voices from the heavens which shout out to tell us that *now* is the time to sell. You have to make that decision alone and at best it is going to be nothing more than a good guess.

By cutting your losses early, you can afford to be wrong many times. By clinging to a loser, you may find your investment capital deteriorates to such a point that one mistake can end your venture into the stock market.

You can give your broker an order to sell if your stock declines to a certain price, so that you don't have to watch the market hour to hour or day to day. Such an instruction is called a *stop loss* order.

Leave Them Even If You Love Them

While a stock is rising, there is no logical reason to sell. Let it continue to appreciate. Ideally, it will go up steadily over a number of weeks, months, or years. If it doubles or triples in value, it will eradicate a host of 15 percent to 20 percent losses taken on your bad choices.

But the stock market is cruel and viciously swift. Gains that have been built up over months can be wiped out in hours. So you can't be afraid to sell out to protect some of those gains.

For example, as your stock moves to higher prices, fix in your mind a price 15 percent to 20 percent below its current price at which you will sell if the stock begins to drop. Then sell if the stock falls to that level! For example, if the stock price is $25, agree with yourself that you will cash out if the price falls to $21. Again, give yourself a band of prices in which you will feel comfortable with the stock bouncing. In this case, from $25 to $21⅛. Once it drops below that limit—sell! If the stock moves higher, move your sell price higher. Generally allow a wider band for higher price stocks, as 15 percent of $50 is obviously more than 15 percent of $25.

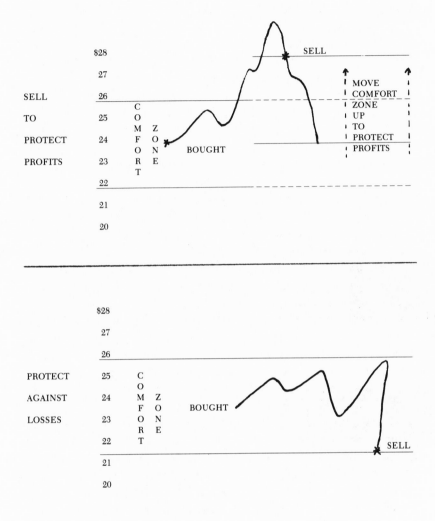

STOCK PRICE

Don't let tax considerations dictate your buy/sell policy. Certainly it is more advantageous to earn a long-term rather than a short-term gain. But you, as an individual, are in the game with

121

a number of investors, like foreigners and pension funds, who play by a different set of tax rules, and they will take their gains and losses without regard to time limits.

When to Fire Your Broker

Your stockbroker isn't someone you need to like, or someone you feel good about helping, or someone with whom you enjoy talking, or even someone your friends believe is prestigious. Your stockbroker is someone who can help you make money. If he isn't, *fire him!*

There is a story about a stockbroker's client who nearly died from an inaccurate prescription that his physician had given him. Asked by his broker one night over dinner which physician he was now seeing, the client replied that he hadn't changed. "After all," he explained, "I like the guy. We play tennis together, and everyone makes mistakes." At that moment, the broker understood why his client had never left him. Even though his account had done miserably, the relationship had been pleasant over a number of years. They ate dinner together occasionally. They had wonderful conversations. They played tennis and were friends. But for all this congeniality, the client's account had lost half its value. The relationship would probably endure until the client lost everything.

If this were unusual, it wouldn't be mentioned. Unfortunately, it is not at all uncommon to find relationships of this sort between client and broker. The reasons are many, but mostly emotional. *Money,* after all, is an intimate subject. It is hard to find a good broker and once you have found one—even though he has faults—it sometimes is easier to live with those faults than to begin the search anew.

Take a hard-nose, businesslike approach to the management of your investment capital and fire your broker: (1) if you aren't making money, (2) if you aren't getting the information or attention you require, (3) if he isn't knowledgeable about the investment area in which you are interested, and (4) if you have a chance to work with someone better.

If you feel you deserve better but don't know where to turn, talk discreetly to your broker's office manager. He understands each of his brokers as well as anyone and can probably provide you with a better match. If you are looking for your first stockbroker, also talk with office managers. Otherwise, if you simply walk or call in, you will wind up with whomever is on call that day. Because you represent potential commissions, it is unlikely that broker will give you up to someone more qualified to help you, and a miserable experience could be brewing from the beginning.

Don't Paddle Against the Current

When the stream is briskly moving in one direction, it is a difficult struggle to go against it. If the stock market is sliding downward, don't buy stocks! The stock of the best company in the world will probably go down if the stock market in general is going down. You have to be very lucky to pick the exceptions. Conversely, if the market is strong, it is very easy to pick winners. There is a theory called *random walk* which, in essence, says that you are as likely to pick a winning stock by randomly selecting stocks from the pages of the newspaper as by doing the analysis that high-priced securities researchers perform.

This theory has validity, and you can apply it by making your purchases of common stocks after a trend up or down has been confirmed, rather than in anticipation of a turn. Let someone else take the biggest risks. Time your purchases to confirmed stock market moves.

When Your Doctor Becomes a Stock Market Expert—Sell!

Investing is not easy. When it becomes too easy, you had better watch out. There is a story that Joseph Kennedy sold all of his common stock holdings before Black Friday when his shoeshine boy began giving him stock tips.

The lesson to be learned from this is that, if you are investing in gold or real estate or stocks because it is an easy way to make money, the honeymoon is probably about to end. No trend goes on forever. By the time your busy doctor "understands" the investment, that opportunity is nearly over. The reason some people get rich is that they change direction before the rest.

Rumors and Other Reasons to Buy Stocks

The most successful investors are readers. They spot investment trends, danger signals, and the opportunities, while most of us who read the same magazines and newspapers read right by them. Our free press is loaded with information that can turn thoughtful readers into shrewd investors, and the material is not limited to the business section. As an investor, you should read news with this thought: what industry or company is likely to benefit or be hurt by this event (or chain of events)?

When you read investment material, don't settle for one source of ideas. No investment firm has all the good ideas. Consider new approaches. Circumstances change with time. To see just how much, pick up some investment books written just ten years ago. Be prudent and selective in your choices, but always be willing to expand your breadth of knowledge. Listen to rumors but act on facts. A rumor may lead you to an excellent investment idea, though by itself it might be worth nothing at all.

The Numbers Game

As at the racetrack, the more tickets you buy, the greater the chances of winning. Diversify, diversify, diversify! Don't get caught up in the thousand-share syndrome unless you can afford to own lots of different thousand-share pieces. Instead, own a couple hundred shares of many different stocks. By diversifying in this manner, you keep yourself from getting badly hurt in any one investment that goes the wrong way and improve your chances of owning stocks that could become winners. Something is always happening to keep your investing interesting because you have stocks in many different industries, each, hopefully, with good potential.

A compelling reason to adhere to this rule comes from *Forbes* magazine. "If you could buy *just one stock* which would it be? Every year the magazine puts that question to a group of intrepid investment professionals. In 1980, a banner year for the Market, five of the nine souls brave enough to participate lost money."

Diversification puts the odds in your favor.

9

Putting It All Together

What follows are guidelines about steps you should take to put together your personal investment program.

Liquid Assets

Before you begin any investment program it is mandatory that you store enough money in an easy-access type of account to take care of potential short-term money needs. The amount varies based on your spending habits, but it will always count in the thousands of dollars. This is the money you can get to quickly to pay unexpected bills, take trips, or replace broken refrigerators. It should not be used to buy investments whose basic value fluctuates substantially from the purchase price. When short-term interest rates are high, money market funds, T-Bills, Federal Farm Credit Bank notes, six-month C.D.'s, or commercial paper are ideal tools for you to use.

If your joint taxable income is high your liquid assets should be in "limited maturity" tax-free bond funds or short-term tax-exempt notes. The higher your tax bracket, the greater the reason to do this. Maturities should never exceed six months.

SHORT-TERM	INTERMEDIATE-TERM	LONG-TERM
40 Percent Tax Bracket and up		
(Joint taxable income of about $36,000 plus)		
Limited Maturity Municipal Bond Fund	Municipal Notes Intermediate-Term	Municipal Bonds and Unit Trusts
BANS/TANS/PHAs (short)	Municipal Bond Trusts	Municipal Bond Funds
		Real Estate Limited Partnerships
39 Percent Tax Bracket and lower		
Money Market Funds	Thirty-Month C.D.'s	Corporate Bonds
Six-Month C.D.'s	T-Notes	Preferred Stocks
C.D. Unit Trusts	Agency Paper	Corporate Bond Funds and Unit Trusts
T-Bills, U.S. Agency Paper		U.S. Government Treasury or Agency Bonds
		Four-year-plus C.D.'s

When short-term rates fall below credit union or savings and loan passbook rates, the money should be moved back to these kinds of accounts.

Don't be tempted by the lure of higher rates available in longer term securities. They are not liquid asset investments and should never be substitutes for them. Don't ever put yourself in the position of being wrong guessing about the short-term potential of a long-term investment tool.

Own a House

The tax advantages of home ownership, which include your ability to deduct from federal income taxes, the heavy interest payments, real estate taxes, and some energy conservation expenditures, while living in your tax shelter, make home ownership a mandatory investment.

Until you own a home, or have made the decision not to own one, buying money with securities is premature. Save your dollars in short-term investment vehicles until after you move in.

Is There Life After Taxes?

There is absolutely no reason to expose your investment dollars to substantial risk if the IRS is going to be the major benefactor of any gain. Choosing investments on the basis of tax consequence is never wise, but selecting them without regard to taxes is downright silly.

Beat the Bank

Most investors look to securities as a method of beating the bank. Ten percent is twice as attractive as five, and in most times, you don't have to be an investment wizard to find bonds that will return double bank interest.

If your goal is to store money forever and simply accumulate interest, you should move your money from passbook savings into bonds. You give up the certainty that your principal will always be intact. Changing interest rates will cause your principal to fluctuate in value. You gain a fixed higher rate of interest. Buy long-term corporate bonds or U.S. government bonds if you are in the 30 percent tax bracket or less. Buy long-term tax-exempt bonds if you are in a higher tax bracket. The reason you should select long rather than short or intermediate is that you will earn the highest interest rate from the longest running bond.

The sort of investors who are best choosing this investment option are usually older people who have no need to spend their principal. They usually can't spend all the interest that the principal generates. They want their financial life as uncomplicated as possible. They realize that they can beat the bank with bonds and that they will probably not be around when the bond matures. Keeping pace with inflation by choosing investments that have some potential for growth is not as important as the highest possible *current* return on their dollars. Because they never intend to sell them, these investors don't worry about the price gyrations of their bonds as long as the income from them is secure and steady.

Keeping the Principal Stable

For those who can't stomach the ups and downs of the long-term bond market but who need high income and a tax break, single premium tax-deferred annuities are a good answer. Put your money in a single premium tax-deferred annuity and your principal investment will not fluctuate at all. Withdraw once a year on a random basis roughly the amount you are earning in interest. If your withdrawals are done in this fashion, the IRS treats the withdrawals as *return of principal* and you will pay no tax on any amount withdrawn until you have taken out an amount equivalent to what you started with. If you are earning 8 percent annual interest on your single premium tax-deferred annuity of $25,000, you could withdraw 8 percent of $25,000, or $2,000 for twelve and a half years, without paying any taxes. At that point, your investment would still be worth $25,000, but when you withdrew any of that amount, you would have to pay taxes on it just as if it were earnings from employment—ordinary income. You could choose to annuitize then or withdraw the $25,000 over a number of years to minimize the tax bite. Each single premium tax-deferred annuity has slightly different rules. Check those before you proceed. For certain people, they are unbeatable.

The Easy Options Are Over

Most people can't afford the luxury of parking money in semipermanent investments. Prudence also calls for a certain amount of diversification among securities based on age, income, and financial goals. While long-term bonds may be better than passbook savings accounts, and single premium tax-deferred annuities ideal places to store money for some, they are not the answer for the majority.

Keep Your Bond Maturities In Sight

Bonds should be part of your securities mix if the interest rate paid by good quality bonds is attractive and the maturities reasonably short term. Money doubles at these rates in this amount of time.

AFTER TAX RATE OF INTEREST	NUMBER OF YEARS
8%	9
10	7
15	5

Doubling your money in less than ten years is a worthy investment objective, and so if you can get these rates, take them with some of your money. Fixed returns act as a ballast in your investment portfolio. If you can't get favorable rates, don't be lured into longer term bonds or less yielding investments, or lesser quality investments. No one knows what is going to happen twenty or thirty years from now, so why buy bonds whose maturities extend that far? You have a better chance of guessing what your life and the world will be like three to seven years from now. Pick maturities in that range. If bank certificates are the highest yielding three- to seven-year investments, choose them over bonds.

THE PROBLEM WITH FIXED INCOME INVESTMENTS

The problem with any fixed income investment is the cancer called inflation, which destroys the future purchasing power of your money. That is why it is so essential that your money always be placed in the most advantageous investments. That is the reason you must *manage* the buying power of your money rather than let your money sit. Inflation is the reason your education about buying the most money with your money is a never-ending one. And it is the reason you must be an *active* money manager. It is not enough to make single money management decisions and sit on them. Inflation doesn't rest. It is constantly on the attack. The battle against inflation will not be won by defensive actions alone. By putting your money advantageously to work *you* take the offense.

LOOK FOR GROWTH

Common stocks, real estate, and oil and gas limited partnerships offer growth opportunities.

Diversify, Diversify, Diversify!!!

Your investment portfolio should never be too heavily weighted in one area of investment or any single security. You expose yourself to too much risk and too little opportunity to be right. The greater the number of common stocks you own, for example, the more chances you have to be right. We all make mistakes. Spread your bets and allow the law of averages to operate. If you own some "lighting stocks," that is, oil and gas companies that could make big finds or drug companies that could discover the next wonder cure or buy out candidates, the chance of explosive growth is possible.

Know Where You Are Going

If you don't know the answers to these questions, no one is going to be able to help you satisfy your investment goals.
1. Why are you investing?
2. What are your objectives?
3. What rate of return do you expect?
4. How much risk are you willing to take?
5. How much time will you commit to investing?

10

Do It Now!

Paul Revere galloped through sleeping Massachusetts towns shouting "The British are coming!" Some people got the word and others slept right through one of America's most historic moments.

Today over 100 billion dollars is invested in money market funds and similar investments earning historically high rates of interest. Yet while this is happening over 700 billion dollars is sleeping in low-yielding passbook savings accounts. Some people haven't got the word. Perhaps some of that money is yours. And that makes no sense!

Today many investors know enough about managing their investment programs to pay significantly fewer tax dollars to the IRS than they did before. Perhaps you could too.

Today there are investment tools nearly any middle-class American can use—and that is the point of this book. There are a number of things most investors don't need to know about investing—*How to Buy Money* doesn't talk about them. The focus, instead, is on investment tools and strategies that are being used right now by investors whose circumstances are no different from yours. You must wake up to the notion that your money could be working harder and smarter than it is.

I like to conclude my money management seminars by telling the audience that 10 percent of them probably know everything I've said and don't need to change a thing about managing their savings program. For those people the seminar was a good experience because it is an affirmation that they are doing all they can. Another 10 percent will be so moved by what they've heard that they will take immediate steps to improve their investment posture. For those people the seminar will contribute materially to their financial well-being. The remaining 80 percent vow that they will do something to improve their investment situation but will put it off. Next year at this time nothing will have changed. What I *hope* is to be persuasive enough to get some of the people in the 80 percent group to do something positive for themselves. If you want to be among them you have to begin today! Henry Ford said, "You can't build a reputation on what you are going to do." So do it!

I began this book by describing an investment called the *equity unit trust*. There were two reasons for doing that. The first was to alert you to the notion that as an investor you will continually be confronted with new and seemingly complicated investment products. The second reason was to make you aware that these investments will not seem as complicated if you have a fundamental understanding of traditional investments. This is what *How to Buy Money* is about.

Even as this book goes to print, changes are taking place in our economy that will change the way money is raised in the future. The character of long-term financing in America will surely change if high inflation persists. For example, no long-term lender will settle for interest payments alone. He will demand, and receive, part of the appreciation in price that is brought about by inflation. He must stay even.

If everyone abandons the passbook account in favor of money market funds, we will need to find a new way to finance the construction of family homes. There won't be any money available to lend to home buyers.

If the level of taxation remains high, no one will invest in anything that doesn't offer some tax advantage.

You must be prepared to manage your money in this environment; to live with the rules that exist—not with those you think should exist or those that worked well for you in the past.

As I mentioned at the start, making money is great fun. But because every judgment you make is subjective, it is not easy. You must devote some of your *best* energy and some of your *freshest* moments to your personal financial program. What good does it do you to earn money if it all slides away because you manage it so poorly?

I have acquainted you with the tools you will need to use and I've instructed you in their use. Now it is your task to pick them up and use them.

11

How to Buy Money in Everyday English (Glossary)

Whether you sail or ski, practice medicine or argue the law, you are guilty of wielding a specialized language that may baffle those who are not participants. The people who buy money are no different. Wall Street has developed a language of its own and it has only to do with the business of money.

This Glossary has been given special care because it includes all those terms that you must understand to go about the task of buying money. It may be equally important because it excludes all those nice-to-know but seldom-used investment terms with which you will rarely be confronted.

This section will be most useful to you if, after reading it the first time, you will refer to it whenever you are faced with an investment term that doesn't make any sense. Use it as your "Berlitz" language guide to the money market.

ACCRUED INTEREST

This is perhaps the most misunderstood investment concept of all and yet one of the most important to buyers of money. You should know that all bonds and notes accumulate interest each day they exist. Accrued interest is the day-to-day accumulation

139

of interest that is earned but not yet paid. Since most bonds and notes pay interest twice a year, there are only two days a year on which either bonds or notes can be bought or sold without involving accrued interest. On every other day, whoever owns the bond or note is entitled to interest. For example, assume that you sold a bond that pays interest every year on January and July 1. The date you sold the bond to someone else was April 1. In addition to sale price you were entitled to receive interest from the date of your last payment, which was January 1, to the date of sale (settlement date). The buyer is required to advance the interest to you because when the interest payment date next arrives on July 1, he will receive a full six-month payment from the bond issuer. Of that payment, he actually earned interest from April 1 to July 1. The balance will simply reimburse him for the money he advanced to you. This procedure exists because it is an orderly arrangement for the bond issuer who is responsible for making the semiannual interest payments. It would be nearly impossible for the bond issuer to keep track of and make payments of different amounts to the many different people who might own the bond for varying amounts of time during any given six-month period between the interest payment dates. It is much easier to pay whoever is the owner of record on the interest payment date.

A bond buyer should expect to see a charge for accrued interest on his purchase confirmation (bill). Conversely, a bond seller should see a credit. Some brokerage firms don't label the accrued interest figure as clearly as they should, and this inevitably leads to questions because the amount can be substantial at times.

ANNUAL REPORT

It's been estimated that the typical investor spends less time reading the annual reports of companies whose stock he owns, than he spends running marathon races. This is unfortunate, because as a common stock owner, you are a part owner of a corporation and the annual report is the summary of how well your company did in the year just past. If you spend a few minutes studying some key figures and come to use the annual report as a tool for analysis, you might decide to buy more shares of that company or sell those that you own. Investment decisions should be made rationally rather than emotionally. The annual report is a good place to begin a rational analysis of your investment.

The annual report consists of two parts, which most people understand, and one other which this section should help you to understand better. The pictures and the chairman's message are a piece of cake. The numbers can be a challenge. Those numbers are broken down into an *income statement*, which shows the extent of the company's profit or loss, and a *balance sheet*, which shows what a company owns and owes. *Footnotes* describe other important information which can affect profits.

How to Read a Financial Report Here are some "number" items which are important parts of the annual report:

Profits. Not only is it important to know whether they went up or down, but you should try to figure out why. One way is to compute the profit margin. That is found by dividing the net income by the sales. Compare that to previous years. Are the profit margins growing? Also look at the company's expenses: the cost of goods sold, which are the selling and administrative expenses, plus interest and taxes. Compare costs to sales for a number of years. Are they rising?

If you really want to do an analytical job, compare your company with others in the same field.

Debt. Compare long-term debt to shareholders' equity. If profits are low, debt is going to be hard to pay, and dividends that are paid for after debt might be in trouble.

Extraordinary items: Be aware if profits are the result of special nonrecurring sales.

If you want to go further, two booklets which are quite helpful are *How to Read a Financial Statement* from Merrill Lynch, Pierce, Fenner and Smith, and *What Else Can Financial Statements Tell You?* from the American Institute of Certified

Public Accountants (AICPA), 1211 Avenue of the Americas, New York, New York 10036.

A book called *Securities Analysis* (see Bibliography) is considered by investment professionals as the bible. It is used to train people in the field, yet one doesn't need a financial background to understand it.

This detailed explanation was not intended to lead you to believe that making proper investment decisions requires considerable time-consuming analysis and the mind of a computer. Most investors rely on the analysis done by security research professionals. The most widely used independent research firms are Standard and Poor's Corporation and Value Line. Most libraries and brokerage offices can provide you with their research reports on companies in which you have an interest.

Brokerage firms, themselves, employ some of the most talented securities research professionals who write publicly available reports on a wide variety of companies. These reports can be obtained from the brokerage firms by simply asking. Since not all brokerage firms prepare research reports on all companies, you may need to ask more than one. Keep in mind also that different firms will have different opinions about the same company.

BEARER BOND

All municipal (tax-free) bonds will be sent to you in this form unless you specify otherwise. Many U.S. government securities are also sold in this way. They are called bearer bonds because they don't have the name of the owner printed on them. They are like dollar bills: whoever has them in his possession is taken to be the owner.

They are also called *coupon bonds* because small coupons are attached to the bond. These can be clipped from (cut off) the bond and turned over to a bank to receive the interest payment on or after the date specified on the coupon. Be aware that an unredeemed coupon won't earn additional interest. Also, be sure to keep some proof of your bearer bond purchase, such as the confirmation or the carbonized paper with your name printed on it that is attached to the bond when it is delivered to you. That paper is a copy of the delivery instructions and contains a detailed description of the bond, as well, and your name and address. Without the proof of purchase it will be impossible to sell the bond through a reputable bank or brokerage firm.

Many people prefer to leave their bonds in their account at their brokerage firm. The coupons are clipped when due and the interest checks mailed to them by the brokerage firm. Generally, this is a safer and more convenient method of maintaining a securities portfolio. Currently this is provided as a free service by most brokerage firms.

BID AND ASKED

Bid is the price you get when you sell your security at the going market price, which is referred to as simply "the market." For actively traded securities, the gap between the bid and ask price is very small. Over-the-counter stocks and most bonds have a wider gap. Brokers refer to the gap as a spread. The reason for the spread is that the securities dealer that handles or *makes the market* for an over-the-counter stock or bond assumes the price fluctuation risk during the period he owns the security. By taking it into his account at the lower price (bid), and selling it at a higher price (ask), he is able to protect himself from some of the risk of the stock or bond dropping in price after he purchased it from the customer.

CAPITAL GAIN OR CAPITAL LOSS

Profits and losses realized from the sale of securities are called capital gains and losses and are taxed differently than income from employment, dividends, and interest. The tax treatment of long-term capital gains is more favorable than of short-term gains because Congress has sought to encourage *investment* in American business as opposed to short-term *trading* in stocks and bonds. The precise treatment varies from time to time as the mood of the Congress shifts. The surest way of dating this book would be to describe today's tax laws on capital gains. The correct current information is widely available.

CASH SALE

The normal brokerage transaction requires settlement in five business days or one calendar week. That is referred to as a *regular way* transaction. It is possible to ask for a *cash*, or *next day* settlement, before the sale or purchase takes place. To enable the broker to fill this order, he must be able to find someone willing to take the other side of the trade. Usually, the seller must make a nominal price concession to the buyer (twelve and a half cents per share).

CERTIFICATES

This is the piece of paper that represents the stock, bond, or other security you purchased. It is usually a fancy watermarked document with language that describes the security on the front side and the form necessary for its sale on the reverse. After purchase of the security it normally takes the brokerage firm two to four weeks to deliver it to you. Many individuals prefer to leave their certificates with their brokerage firm. When securities are sold, they must be delivered to the brokerage firm within five business days—signed in the appropriate place on the back in the same way it is registered on the face.

DAY ORDER

Unless you specify otherwise, the order you place with your broker to buy or sell a security at a specific price will be good for that day only. At the end of trading that order will be canceled. It is possible, however, to place an order to buy or sell a security at a specified price that will be valid until you cancel it. That is called a *good 'til cancel* (GTC), or *open order*. During the time

144

the order is in force, it will be reduced in price automatically to take in account any dividends paid. For example, if you have a GTC order to buy 100 shares of McDonald's Corporation at $50.00 a share, and McDonald's pays a 50¢ dividend, your order will be changed to buy 100 shares at $49.50 unless you specify at the time you enter the order that you don't want the price lowered. That is termed *do not reduce.* Some brokerage firms will automatically cancel a GTC order after some specified period of time. A notice indicating that the GTC order has been placed is mailed to the customer. On that notice an automatic cancellation date, if any exists, will be given.

DEBIT BALANCE

Any money owed to the brokerage firm is called a *debit balance.* Any money owed you is called a *credit balance.* A brokerage firm client who has a *margin account,* that is, someone who is borrowing money from the brokerage firm to help pay for his securities, will have a debit balance. On that amount, he is charged interest by the brokerage firm. The firm holds the securities as collateral for the loan and allows the interest to accrue rather than send a monthly bill for the interest charge. The interest rate charged changes with the prevailing interest rates. The brokerage firm itself borrows the money before the money is lent to the firm's clients. The brokerage firm makes a profit by charging some amount above its cost to its clients. Usually, the larger the debit balance owed by a client, or the more active his account, the lower the rate of interest he will be charged—and of course, vice versa.

There are U.S. government rules called *Regulation T* and *Regulation U* having to do with margin accounts. Regulation T governs the amount that can be loaned by brokerage firms to customers based on the value of their securities. Regulation U governs the amount that can be loaned by banks to their customers for the purchase of securities. The NYSE and the brokerage firms themselves also have rules to regulate the amount of credit that can be extended.

145

DISCRETIONARY ACCOUNT

This is an account in which the customer gives the broker or an investment adviser or someone else the right to make purchases and sales of securities on the customer's behalf. This can be done only when the customer signs a specific agreement, usually called a *limited power of attorney*. Unless a customer has given this written authority to his broker, all transactions must be done with the knowledge and approval of the customer.

DIVERSIFICATION

Spreading investment dollars among different types of investments, different kinds of securities, and securities of different companies is called diversifying your investments. While diversification is wise, overdiversification can be unwise. The most common way of expressing this strategy is: don't put all your eggs in one basket. If something happens to that basket, you may lose everything. The corollary to this rule is that too many baskets may become a juggling act. You want to be able to properly handle them. It's important to stay on top of your investments by following developments that can affect them. Achieving a balance between proper diversification and a mumbo-jumbo collection of securities should be your goal.

DOLLAR COST AVERAGING

This is the practice of buying a particular common stock or mutual fund with the same number of dollars at periodic intervals. Because shares are purchased both when they are priced high and low, an averaging of price occurs over time. This method is commonly used by investors who are allowed to invest a certain percentage of their salary in the common stock of their company. It is a savings program using common stock as the savings tool. Obviously, a larger number of shares are purchased when their price is low than when it is high.

DOW JONES INDUSTRIAL AVERAGE

This is the most widely used figure to gauge whether the stock market has had a good day or bad day. It is the average of thirty different industrial stocks traded on the NYSE. They are:

Allied Chemical	IBM
Aluminum Co.	International Harvester
American Brands	International Paper
American Can	Johns-Manville
American Tel & Tel	Merck
Bethlehem Steel	Minnesota Mining
Du Pont	Owens-Illinois
Eastman Kodak	Procter & Gamble
Exxon	Sears Roebuck
General Electric	Standard Oil of Cal.
General Foods	Texaco
General Motors	Union Carbide
Goodyear	United Technologies
Inco	U.S. Steel
Westinghouse Electric	Woolworth

These companies are considered leaders in their industries. Their common stocks are broadly distributed among individual and institutional investors and have a large market valuation.

To arrive at the Dow Jones Industrial Average, the prices of the stocks are totaled and then divided by a number other than thirty so as to take account of the stock splits and substitutions that have occured over the fifty-plus year history of the Dow Jones Industrial Average.

The direction of the stock market is as steady as a weather vane. While there are other gauges, such as the NYSE Composite Index, which better point the direction of the market, none is more widely followed than the Dow Jones Industrial Average.

EX-DIVIDEND

Ex means "without." When a stock trades Ex-Dividend, it is trading without the dividend. To be entitled to the dividend you must be listed on the company's record books as a shareholder of record. Since the normal settlement date for a stock transaction is five business days after the day the purchase takes place (trade date), the rule says that you will be listed as a shareholder of record on the settlement date. If you are not entitled to be listed as a shareholder of record, you are not entitled to the dividend.

Five business days before the shareholder of record date occurs, purchasers of the stock are advised that they will not be entitled to the next dividend, because this date is called the Ex-Dividend date. So if you are buying a stock to receive the next dividend, be sure to ask about the Ex date. This means that as a purchaser on or after the Ex-Dividend date you will not be entitled to receive the next dividend. The stock is said to trade Ex-Dividend. For example, if you were to buy 100 shares of McDonald's common stock before the Ex date, you would be a shareholder of record and entitled to the dividend. After the Ex date, you would not be entitled.

GOLD

Gold, the price of oil, and inflation have tended to keep pace. Therefore, it is not an unreasonable place to put some of your money. From $40 an ounce in 1972 to $800 an ounce in 1980 and all around since, gold has attracted the attention of many investors. Some believe the price is linked to world unrest and others to the erratic monetary policies of the Federal Reserve. Whatever the reason, if you want to own gold here are some of the ways to go about it.

Coins. Banks, currency dealers, and brokerage firms will sell you such coins as South African Krugerrands, Canadian Maple Leafs, Mexican 50 pesos, and Austrian 100 coronas. These gold bullion coins typically sell at a small premium to the value of their gold content. They are easy to store, attractive, rarely counterfeited, and easy to sell.

Gold Bars. Available in various sizes and forms, a kilo bar, 32.15 ounces, is a standard piece of trade. Most dealers will store the metal for you. Should you take delivery, you will need to have your bullion assayed (evaluated as to quality and weight) before you can sell it. This can be expensive and I recommend that if you are buying it to trade, you not take delivery.

Gold Certificates. It is also possible to buy relatively small dollar amounts ($50–$5,000) of gold through many banks and brokers. Rather than receiving the metal, your ownership is evidenced by a certificate of ownership. This is the most convenient and usually least expensive way of participating in the metals markets.

INSTITUTIONAL INVESTOR

Pension funds, mutual funds, banks, insurance companies, universities, charitable foundations, corporations, or other non-individual investors are called institutional investors. These organizations have a great deal of money to invest, and generally buy and sell large holdings of stocks and bonds. For this reason, their actions have an important effect on the state of the market. It is possible to determine institutional interest in a particular common stock by looking through the monthly *Standard and Poor's Stock Guide*, which reports the number of institutional investors that own each stock, as well as the number of shares they own.

INTEREST

Interest is the rent paid by a borrower for the use of money. There are two major types of interest. *Simple interest* is where the rate is always computed on the original principal. Simple interest is used in computing the interest on U.S. government, corporate, and municipal bonds. *Compound interest* is where the interest is computed and added to the principal periodically. Future interest is then computed on the larger amount. Series EE bonds and tax-deferred annuities are examples of investments that compound interest.

JOINT OWNERSHIP

The most common way for a husband and wife to own securities is called *Joint Tenancy with Right of Survivorship.* Its advantage is that when one of the owners dies, the property passes to the survivor without the expense or delay of probate. Assuming one has a good relationship with the other joint owner and his total estate is moderate in size, JTWROS is normally the best form of ownership. This is also the form of ownership most banks and brokerage firms assume you will select. Therefore, it is often chosen for you. Perhaps it is not best in your case.

An alternate choice is called *Joint Tenancy by the Entirety*. This form of ownership allows the securities to be held in joint names, but at death provides that the share owned by the decedent will not pass directly to the surviving owner but will be disposed of according to that person's will.

Some tax/estate attorneys will advise their clients to buy their securities individually rather than keeping them in a joint account. Tax and estate planning is a necessity for people whose incomes or estates push them into the upper middle class. A qualified tax and estate attorney will be best able to determine how securities should be owned for you if this is your circumstance.

LOAD

Means "sales charge." No load means no sales charge. There are sometimes back-end loads as well as front-end loads—the former being a sales charge levied when the security is sold, and the latter when it is purchased. Load is not the term used to describe the brokerage commission charged on normal buy-and-sell transactions. Rather, load applies to a buried or hidden charge associated with a mutual fund or a tax-deferred annuity.

LONG

A security that is held in your brokerage account for you is referred to as being *long* in your account. It is the other side of being *short* in your account—which means that the security should be in your account but isn't.

MARKET ORDER

An order to purchase or sell a security at its current price. This sort of order contrasts to a *limit order*, which specifies a price for the purchase or sale. The market price will usually be close to the last reported price at which the security was sold.

MONEY MARKET FUNDS

Among the best savings account alternatives available, money market funds are pools of money used to purchase higher yielding securities such as commercial paper (unsecured corporate IOUs), bank certificates of deposit, government and Treasury securities. Most funds allow their investors to write checks against their accounts as long as the checks are in the amounts of $500 or more. Minimum initial investments vary from $1,000 to $5,000. Shares can be redeemed at any time. The value of the shares is usually set at $1 each. While the value of the securities within the fund varies from day to day, the fund managers adjust the yield rather than the share value. Because the securities in the fund have very short maturities, the fund's net asset value changes only slightly. The benefit: in periods of high short term interest rates the return available on money market funds will be very high. The drawback: these funds are not insured by the FDIC or FSLIC as are your dollars, to certain limits, which are held in savings accounts in banks and savings and loan associations.

MUTUAL FUND

This is a company that consists of a portfolio of securities of other corporations. These securities are bought and sold by the managers of the mutual fund based on their judgment of what are proper investment decisions. Shares of the fund may be purchased by individuals and their value will fluctuate daily with the value of the underlying securities. There are mutual funds that consist of common stocks, and others that are made up of bonds. Within these groupings, each fund has its own objectives: for example, trading profits, long-term growth, emerging growth issues, utility stocks that pay high dividends. These mutual funds, whose shares are traded on the stock exchanges, are called *closed-end funds*. This means that only a certain number of shares exist. In order to purchase these, you must buy the shares through a brokerage firm and pay a brokerage commission. *Open-end funds* issue new shares to new buyers and cancel out the shares of the sellers. Unlike the closed-end funds there is no limit to the number of shares open-end funds can offer. Those open-end mutual fund shares purchased through a brokerage firm are called *load funds*. The load is the brokerage fee. Those purchased directly through the mutual fund are no load as they involve no sales fee. The Wiesenberger mutual fund book and Johnson's mutual fund chart book are available at good libraries and show the past performance of all funds and provide other useful evaluating information about mutual funds.

ODD LOTS

Some number less than the standard trading block referred to as a round lot. When referring to common stocks an odd lot is any number of shares less than one hundred. Corporate and municipal bonds also trade in one hundred-bond round lots. Many preferred stocks trade in ten-share round lots. It used to be common practice for a brokerage firm to charge an *odd lot differential* fee for handling odd lot transactions. That was because the trades weren't handled on the exchanges but by separate private firms. Now a few of the major brokerage firms perform this function themselves and waive the odd lot fee.

OPTIONS

An option is the right to buy or sell one hundred shares of stock at a specified price within a certain period of time. The right to buy is called a *call* option. The right to sell is called a *put* option.

If you are a gambler options offer you the chance to place a small bet on stock prices and make a bundle or lose only the amount of the bet. If you are a conservative investor and own some stocks, options can be a hedge against sharp moves in those stocks. Options can even produce some additional income for stock owners.

The most common option strategy is to write (sell) call options on stocks you already own. That is called *covered writing*. The money you receive by selling calls gives you some additional income. It also gives you some downside price protection. For example, let's say you bought 100 shares of a stock at $25 and sold an April 30 call. For selling the call you receive $3 per share. That means that you have reduced your true cost from $25 to $22. (Be sure to count commission expenses to get *your* true costs.)

The call buyer is betting that the price of the stock will go up before the expiration date in April. If it does, the option price will go up. If it goes down, the price will go down. Why buy an option? The option buyer can double his money overnight, but he could as easily lose his entire investment. It is as close to gambling as you can come on Wall Street.

Another strategy is buying puts which can provide a hedge against a stock price collapse. The put buyer has the right to sell the stock at the agreed upon *strike* price. So if the stock declines in value you have the right to sell it at the higher agreed upon price. If the stock price rises and you sell it, your profit is reduced by the amount you paid to buy the put.

Puts and calls are only two types of options and these strategies are only a few of the ones available to you. As you see, the world of options is far from basic investing. It is an investment form best used by someone who considers himself a knowledgeable investor.

OVER-THE-COUNTER

Nearly all U.S. government securities and municipal bonds are bought and sold over the counter. Common stock shares of smaller companies that haven't yet qualified for listing on the major stock exchanges and some small issues of corporate bonds also trade in this market. It is a brokerage firm-to-brokerage firm telephonically connected market. Video display screens show the brokers their competitor's prices for each security.

POINT

When referring to the price of shares of a stock a point means one dollar. Most stocks trade in ⅛ point fractions of $1.00. So if a stock rises $1.25, it is up 1¼ points. Bonds are different. Since bond prices are quoted in percentage figures with 100 equaling $1,000.00 and 50 equal to $500.00, a point difference in a bond is one percentage point, or $10.00. So if a bond is quoted at 89¼, its price is $892.50. If the quote is 90½, the price is $905, and so on.

PORTFOLIO

A fancy term that means one's security holdings. Whether it consists of five shares of one company and a bond of another, or thirty different issues totaling several million dollars, each is considered an investment portfolio.

PRIME RATE

The rate at which banks loan money to their best customers. It is a gauge of the economy's prevailing interest rate. When the prime rate is high, generally all interest rates are high. When it falls on a week-to-week basis, generally all interest rates come down. The cost of money directly affects the economy as business and individuals tend to buy less when money is expensive to buy, and more when it is cheap.

PROXY

Written authorization on the part of the stockholder to vote his shares at the annual shareholders' meeting.

154

RALLY

A healthy rise in price of a security or a general market. If one says, "The bond market rallied," one means that prices of bonds generally moved higher.

SEC

The Securities and Exchange Commission is the U.S. government regulatory agency that oversees securities transactions. It is the investors' watchdog and a body the investor can turn to when he can't get a problem solved by the brokerage firm with which he is dealing.

The address is: Office of Consumer Affairs, Securities and Exchange Commission, 500 North Capitol Street, N.W., Washington, D.C. 20549.

SHORT SALE

Brokers refer to securities that are in a brokerage account as being *long* in the account. Those that should be there but aren't are referred to as being *short*. A short sale literally means that the security has been sold but wasn't in the account to sell.

Short selling is a strategy that allows an investor to take advantage of the declining price of a security. For example, if you believe that Ford common stock will decline in value, you can sell it today at its current price. Let's say it's $50. If you are right and the stock declines to $40 a share you will make $10 a share—less brokerage fees. There are, of course, strict rules that govern the amount of money that must be in your brokerage account to do a short sale. Also, the brokerage firm must deliver the stock you sold to whomever purchased it. To do that the brokerage firm will borrow the stock on your behalf. Short selling is not for everyone. It can be very risky and is best done by experienced investors.

SIPC

This is the brokerage industry's answer to FDIC and FSLIC. However, it is *not* a government agency. It is the Securities Investor Protection Corporation, a nonprofit brokerage community corporation created by an act of Congress to promote investor confidence in the nation's securities markets. This protection is against theft and loss of securities held in your brokerage account only. It does not protect against bad investment decisions, bond coupons that were not clipped by mistake, or lost interest. Protection is $500,000 per customer of which no more than $100,000 can be used for cash claims. The source of the money is assessments on SIPC members and the interest this money earns on investments in U.S. government securities. If the need arises, the Securities and Exchange Commission has the authority to lend SIPC up to 1 billion dollars. Most major firms carry additional private insurance as well, which boosts the protection limit per account considerably.

SOPHISTICATED INVESTOR

What brokers commonly call someone with a lot of money. It has been reported that J. D. Rockefeller said that if you have 5 million dollars making 1 million dollars more is easy. The difficult money to make is $1,000 when you start with $500.

STOCK SPLIT

Less expensive stocks usually have a wider market appeal. So the Boards of Directors of companies will, from time to time, divide the number of shares they have outstanding to lower their share price. For example, 100 shares of a $50 per share stock will become 200 shares of a $25 stock. This is referred to as a two for one split. As you can see from the example, the true value of the holding did not change—only the arrangement. It's much like exchanging a ten-dollar bill for two fives. Psychologically, a stock split has more value as investors tend to react favorably and bid up the price of the stock after a split is announced.

STREET NAME

Securities left with the brokerage firm are not held in the owner's name. They are actually held on the record books of the issuing companies in the name of the brokerage firm. This is called the *street name.* Most securities held by a brokerage firm are held in vaults at the firm's main office. Many people mistakenly believe that the securities are at the branch office with which they deal and can be picked up at that office. As this is not true and as securities must be reregistered when a customer requests that they be delivered to him from the brokerage firm, a two-to-four-week handling period is normally involved.

TECHNICAL RESEARCH

In contrast to *fundamental research and analysis,* which has to do with the evaluation of a company's prospects based on its sales, assets, earnings potential, markets, products, and management among other similar considerations, *technical research* is a study of the market price action of the stock alone. It is sort of witch-doctory to most investors who aren't able to recognize with the same confidence the clues to future price action that the technicians find in the patterns and trends of stock price charts. Yet, technical analysis has a broad base of followers and many books are available on the subject. For the list see the Bibliography.

TRANSFER AGENT

A transfer agent maintains the record of the name and address of each common share or registered bond owner. The agent is usually a bank which is paid a fee by the corporation to handle such business. Some corporations act as their own transfer agent. When securities are sold, the transfer agent collects from the selling brokerage firm the old certificate and issues a new one. There is great inconsistency in the competency of the hundreds of transfer agents throughout the country, causing the time difference in transfer to vary substantially for each security.

UNIT TRUSTS

These are portfolios of specific investments that are rarely changed. They are referred to as unmanaged portfolios. A certain number of shares or units of each portfolio are available for sale when the unit trust is brought to market. When these are sold the subscriptions are closed. The units can then be bought and sold in the secondary market, which is generally maintained by the brokerage firm that originally assembled the unit trust. Advantages to the investor: (1) diversification—as each trust is made up of many different securities, (2) ability to purchase $1,000 units rather than those in larger dollar amounts, and (3) no annual management fee. Disadvantages to the investor: (1) the sales charge can be as high as 5 percent per $1,000 unit, and (2) there may be securities in the portfolio which you wouldn't choose to own if you were buying individual securities rather than a preassembled portfolio.

There are unit trust portfolios of six-month certificates of deposit, intermediate-term and long-term municipal and corporate bonds, U.S. government securities, and even utility company common stocks. Dividends are normally paid monthly but can be reinvested in a separate, managed portfolio of the same type of securities through an automatic dividend reinvestment plan.

As the various bonds in the trust mature, your capital will be returned, but if you sell before maturity, just as with any fixed income investment, you may get more or less than your original purchase price.

VOLUME

In addition to wanting to know if the market is up or down and by how much, the next most frequently asked question is about the volume. Volume simply means the total number of shares traded. This figure is also kept of each stock. High volume when the market is sharply up or down is a more meaningful indication of a trend than low or moderate volume.

WALL STREET

There is a Wall Street. It is located at what once was the foot of a wall the Dutch settlers built to keep the cattle in and the Indians out of the young colony called New Amsterdam. Hence, the inspired selection of the name.

As early as the time before the Revolutionary War, Wall Street was the site of a significant number of major historical occurrences. Among them, in a courthouse on Wall Street, John Peter Zenger was acquitted of libel for his anti-British writings. This ruling is given credit for the establishment of freedom of the press in America. The Stamp Act Congress convened on Wall Street, George Washington established his military headquarters there, and on this street the first public reading of the Declaration of Independence took place.

Alexander Hamilton wrote the majority of his *Federalist Papers* in his office at 33 Wall Street, and George Washington was inaugurated as the first American president there. It was on Wall Street that the Supreme Court was created, as well as The Bank of New York. Both American government and commerce can trace some of their origins to Wall Street. As the seat of governmental power moved south to Washington, the seat of financial power became concentrated there. Shares of incoming cargo were bought and sold by merchants on Wall Street, and it was there that the first U.S. government bonds were issued. As early as 1792, the first stock exchange opened on Wall Street. Most of the shares traded then, and even into the early 1800s, were those of banking institutions. Wall Street today is as much a home to the American banking industry as it is to the stock brokerage industry, although most people identify Wall Street only with the work of stocks and bonds. The "Street's" role in American and world trade is ever evolving.

159

Bibliography

If you view *How to Buy Money* as a basic investment course, this section should be regarded as the supplement to what you learned in class. I've broken it down by subject matter. Keep in mind that because the world of investments changes constantly, the best sources for up-to-date information are: the financial section of your newspaper, the *Wall Street Journal, Forbes* magazine, and *Barrons* magazine.

BONDS

The Complete Bond Book. David M. Darst. Mc-Graw-Hill, 1975. A thorough introduction to the bond market. Advice about how to buy and sell as well as how to analyze bonds that fit your needs. It includes many charts, worksheets, and tables you will find interesting.

How to Invest in Bonds. Hugh C. Sherwood. McGraw-Hill, 1974. A good basic introduction to the entire world of fixed income securities. Solid advice about choosing bonds in layman's language.

GENERAL INVESTMENT MATTERS

Sylvia Porter's New Money Book For the 80's. Sylvia Porter. Avon, 1980.

Everyone's Money Book. Jane Bryant Quinn. Delacote Press, 1978.

Successful Investing: A Complete Guide to Your Financial Future. David R. Sargent and the staff of United Business Service. Simon & Schuster, 1979.

All are excellent basic money books that cover a wide range of investment material as well as other money questions. Everyone should own one of these as a basic reference book for money questions.

SECURITY ANALYSIS

The bible of fundamental analysis is *Security Analysis* by Benjamin Graham, *et al.*, McGraw-Hill, 1962. It is deep reading for all but the most serious investor. If you want to read what the professional analysts have to say, this is the book.

The authoritative guide about technical analysis is *Technical Analysis of Stock Trends* by Robert D. Edwards and John McGee, published by McGee. Also very serious and expensive ($40) but the best in my opinion.

TAX SHELTERS

Tax Shelters That Work for Everyone. Judith H. McQuown. McGraw-Hill, 1979. Good basic information about the tax shelters your broker will offer to you.

Tax Shelters, A Complete Guide. Robert and Carol Tannenhauser. Harmony Books, 1978. Also an excellent tax shelter primer. Many brokerage firms provided this book to their account executives so they could learn about tax shelters.

COMMON STOCKS

How to Buy Stocks. Louis Engel with Peter Wyckoff. Bantam, 6th ed., 1977. This is the classic stock market primer. It has sold over 15 million copies. Its clear approach to the subject is one important reason.

Shaking the Money Tree: New Growth Opportunities in Common Stocks. Winthrop Knowlton and John L. Furth. Harper & Row, 1972. Another easy to understand book about picking stocks that fit your objectives.

The Battle for Investment Survival. Gerald M. Loeb. Simon & Schuster, 1935. Another classic. A solid book every serious stock market investor should read.

ESTATE PLANNING

The Complete Estate Planning Guide. Robert Brosterman. New American Library, Mentor Books, 1964. If your broker knows anything about estate planning, it was probably learned from this book. Short of your tax and estate attorney, this book has most of the answers.

Planning an Estate. Harold Weinstock. McGraw-Hill, 1977.

FUN MONEY BOOKS

The Money Masters. John Train. Harper & Row, 1980. How some of the country's most successful investors got that way.

The Only Investment Guide You'll Ever Need. Andrew Tobias. Bantam, 1979. Witty incisive comments about managing money and learning to enjoy the task.

About the Author

Wayne Nelson (a Merrill Lynch vice-president) is called by his peers one of the most creative brokers in the business. Because his approach to money questions is so even-handed he is a widely sought-after speaker at investment seminars. He has influenced the investment lives of thousands of people.